Cambridge English

David McKeegan
Series Editor: Annette Capel

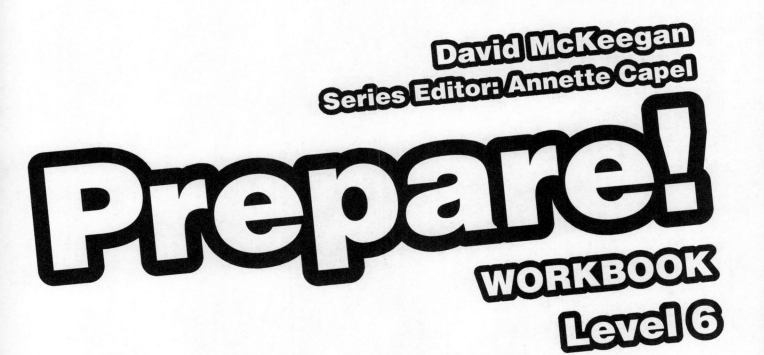

Prepare!
WORKBOOK
Level 6

Cambridge University Press
www.cambridge.org/elt

Cambridge Assessment English
www.cambridgeenglish.org

Information on this title: www.cambridge.org/9780521180320

© Cambridge University Press and UCLES 2015

This publication is in copyright. Subject to statutory exception
and to the provisions of relevant collective licensing agreements,
no reproduction of any part may take place without the written
permission of the publishers.

First Published 2015

20 19 18 17 16 15 14 13

Printed in Great Britain by CPI Group (UK) Ltd, Croydon CR0 4YY

A catalogue record for this publication is available from the British Library

ISBN 978-0-521-18031-3 Student's Book
ISBN 978-1-107-49797-9 Student's Book and Online Workbook
ISBN 978-0-521-18032-0 Workbook with Audio
ISBN 978-0-521-18034-4 Teacher's Book with DVD and Teacher's Resources Online
ISBN 978-0-521-18035-1 Class Audio CDs
ISBN 978-1-107-49794-8 Presentation Plus DVD-ROM

Downloadable audio for this publication at www.cambridge.org/PrepareAudio

The publishers have no responsibility for the persistence or accuracy of URLs
for external or third-party internet websites referred to in this publication, and
do not guarantee that any content on such websites is, or will remain, accurate
or appropriate. Information regarding prices, travel timetables, and other factual
information given in this work is correct at the time of first printing but the
publishers do not guarantee the accuracy of such information thereafter.

Contents

1 New year, new challenge

VOCABULARY   Education: phrasal verbs

1 Match the beginnings and endings of the sentences.

1 I enjoy trying out   ....
2 I think we break up for the summer   ....
3 Daniel hasn't given in   ....
4 I'm going to go for the position   ....
5 Don't put things off for too long   ....
6 I feel that I'm going to get on well   ....
7 The football coach read out the names   ....
8 I'm going to stay behind after   ....
9 Our teacher gave out all   ....
10 I love joining in   ....
11 Don't forget to note down   ....
12 I'm going to try to get in   ....
13 I can't figure out   ....

a school and do some extra work.
b all the details in your book.
c new things.
d on 6 June.
e the new assignments to everyone yesterday.
f his homework yet.
g the school football team this term.
h the answer to this maths problem.
i of everyone in the team.
j or you might never do them.
k at school this year.
l when someone starts singing.
m of team captain.

2 Complete the email with the verbs in the box.

break up   figure out   get in   get on   give out   go for   hand in
join in   note down   put off   stay behind   try out

Hi Jane

I've just started at my new school and it's great. I think I'm going to
¹ .... really well here. There are lots of interesting clubs –
I'm going to ² .... rock climbing this year! I've never done
it before, but it sounds fun so I decided to ³ .... it.

The students in my class are really friendly. A few ⁴ ....
after school to play basketball and they asked me to ⁵ ....
with them. As you know, I'm pretty good at basketball and my new
friends think I will ⁶ .... the school team if I try!

There's a lot more work to do, though. The teachers ⁷ ....
homework every day and we have to ⁸ .... most of it
the next morning. There's always one piece that we can do over the
week, but I try not to ⁹ .... doing it for too long. I have to
remember to ¹⁰ .... everything the teachers say about the
homework , or I forget it. The timetable is quite complicated too, but I'll
¹¹ .... where to go at what time soon, I'm sure!

We ¹² .... on 15 December, so I'll come and visit you then.
Write soon!

Debbie

READING

1 What advice would you give to someone starting
at a new school? Write three ideas.

....
....
....

2 Read the article. Does the author give the same
advice as you?

3 Match these headings to the paragraphs.

1 Get involved!   ....
2 Find out about the school   ....
3 Be a conversation starter   ....
4 Don't be afraid to stand out   ....
5 Pay attention to others   ....
6 Be brave   ....
7 Put on your friendly face   ....

New kid at school?

Going to school in a new town can be pretty stressful. Believe me, I know from experience. Not to worry though, there are ways to get through it! Here are a few tips I've come up with. I hope they help!

A When you go in on your first day at your new school, remember that not everyone is as scary as they seem. Those first few hours are always a bit rough, but don't be afraid or shy. Just go for it! It's nearly always true that most people are nice once you have a chance to talk to them.

B It's likely that your teachers will introduce you to your new classmates, but make sure you personally introduce yourself to the student sitting next to you. Looking for something to talk about? Don't worry! Being new is a great topic. People seem to love talking about where you're from and the school you used to go to.

C Take time to learn the names of other people, and don't forget to take an interest in the person you're talking to. It shows that you're not just concerned about yourself, but also learning about the other person.

D It sounds obvious but it really works: make eye contact with others, smile at them when they look at you and laugh when they say something that's funny or amusing to you. It makes you seem open and easygoing.

E Nobody expects you to know everything about your new school the first day you walk in. There's a huge possibility that your new school will be totally different from the one you just came from. If you have a question, ask it! Don't forget that everyone is new at some point.

F Whether you're entering a new school in the beginning of the year or the middle, the best way to meet new people is by joining in activities like clubs and sports. After school is a time when students with similar interests get together and it's a perfect way to introduce yourself.

G If you are good at a certain sport or do well in a certain subject don't be shy – show it! People are attracted to others with talent, and hiding yours to avoid showing off will only end up hurting you. So if you have a special talent or skill, let people know about it!

4 Complete the summary sentences.

1 People might seem scary at first, but ....
....

2 The fact that you are new can help you ....
....

3 It's a good idea to try to remember ....
....
....

4 You can let people know you are friendly by ....
....

5 You should ask questions about your new school because ....
....

6 The best way to meet new friends is ....
....

7 Don't be afraid to let others know if ....
....

EP **Word profile** *use*

Complete the sentences with the phrases in the box.

> any use   made too much use
> no use   no use   some use

1 I'm sorry, but this information is of
.... to me.

2 You .... of Wikipedia to write your essay!

3 Is this book of .... to you?

4 It's .... worrying about the project – just start it!

5 I think this box could be of .... , maybe as a pencil case.

GRAMMAR Question forms; subject and object questions

1 Match the questions to the answers.

1 What clubs have you joined this term? ......

2 Were you getting ready to go out at 8.00 am this morning? ......

3 What teams did you manage to get in last year? ......

4 Where do you usually go after school? ......

5 How have you changed since you were ten years old? ......

6 Can you swim 100 metres in less than two minutes? ......

7 Do you drink coffee at breakfast? ......

8 Should you spend longer on your homework in the evenings? ......

a The swimming team.

b Only the basketball and photography ones.

c No, I can't.

d I nearly always go straight home.

e Yes, I was.

f Yes, I probably should.

g No, never.

h I've grown much taller!

2 Write the words in the correct order to make questions.

1 you / lived / how long / in your house / have / ?

....

....

2 go / you / did / on holiday / last year / ?

....

....

3 doing / at 8.00 pm last night / you / were / what / ?

....

....

4 both / can / drive / your parents / ?

....

....

5 there / good cafés / are / near your school / any / ?

....

....

6 to do / going / you / are / tomorrow / what / ?

....

....

3 Choose the correct answer to make subject or object questions.

1 Who *sits / does sit* next to you in class?

2 What *watched you / did you watch* on TV last night?

3 What *means 'enrichment' / does 'enrichment' mean*?

4 How *happened / did that happen* to your bike?

5 Who *called you / did call you* during the science class?

6 What *said you / did you say* to the teacher?

7 Where *like you / do you like* to go in the evenings?

8 Who *ate / did eat* all the chocolates?

4 Complete the questions.

0 How many ...*cakes did you make*............... ?
I made three cakes.

1 What sort of concerts .... ?
Dan loves going to jazz concerts in particular.

2 How many students .... ?
I'm not sure, but at least 30 joined the music club.

3 Who .... ?
I phoned Jenny early this morning.

4 Who .... ?
Martin phoned me early this morning.

5 What .... ?
I think this word means *difficult*.

5 Write questions for the answers.

1 Simon got in the swimming team.

.... ?
Simon.

.... ?
The swimming team.

2 Steph does her homework before breakfast.

.... ?
Steph.

.... ?
Before breakfast.

3 My new bike cost €450.

.... ?
€450.

.... ?
My new bike.

4 My sister gave me a bracelet for my birthday.

.... ?
My sister.

.... ?
A bracelet.

6 ⊙ Choose the correct sentence in each pair.

1 a Why they are not here?
  b Why aren't they here?

2 a Is it still available in September?
  b Does it still available in September?

3 a Why it says this?
  b Why does it say this?

4 a Did you had a nice day?
  b Did you have a nice day?

5 a Why did she have to move?
  b Why she had to move?

6 a What language facilities you provide?
  b What language facilities do you provide?

VOCABULARY Education: *-ion* nouns

1 Complete the table with the verb or the noun form of the word.

	Verb	Noun
1	....	action
2	apply	....
3	collect	....
4	communicate	....
5	contribute	....
6	....	decision
7	....	description
8	....	education
9	introduce	....
10	....	invention
11	....	organisation
12	permit	....
13	....	preparation
14	register	....
15	satisfy	....
16	....	suggestion

2 Complete the sentences with a noun from exercise 1.

1 Some say the television was the most important .... of the 20th century.

2 Greg has a large .... of old CDs in his house.

3 You must try harder at school because .... is very important.

4 Have you asked for .... to take the day off school tomorrow?

5 My .... to my first choice of university was accepted.

6 Thank you for your .... to this afternoon's discussion.

7 When does .... for the new English course open?

8 I have a .... – let's join the rock-climbing club.

9 We've made our .... – we're not going on holiday this year.

10 For your homework, write a .... of your favourite building.

WRITING An email (1)

See Prepare to write box, Student's Book page 13.

1 Read the email about Dan's first day at a new school. Tick (✔) the topics he mentions. (Ignore the punctuation.)

1 other students ☐	5 the food ☐
2 the curriculum ☐	6 sports facilities ☐
3 the teachers ☐	7 the building ☐
4 the food ☐	8 the classrooms ☐

2 Read the email again. Some punctuation is incorrect. Find and correct the following.

> 9 capital letters   5 full stops   7 apostrophes

Hi Jan

how are you? My first day at the new school wasnt as bad as I thought it would be. I was really nervous when I arrived in the morning Its a huge grey building that looks like a prison. It's much bigger than our old school, with two big concrete playgrounds. Believe me, it doesnt look very welcoming.

everyone was really friendly, though they seemed genuinely interested in me and wanted to know all about where i came from. So although I was nervous at first, I felt very happy and relaxed by the end of the day. Ive already made new friends

The teachers are OK too, well, most of them are. Our maths teacher seems really strict, but everyone says hes friendly when you get to know him the french teachers name is mr bird. He's the funniest teacher I've ever had. He makes us laugh.

The only thing I didn't like was lunch as the café isn't as good as our old one. Im going to ask Mum to make me a packed lunch to take in that will be much better!

Write soon,

Dan

3 Imagine you have just had your first day at a new school. Choose four topics from exercise 1 and write an email to your friend.

2 Live music

VOCABULARY Music

1 Write the letters in the correct order to make seven different styles of music.

1 L A C S L I C A S ....
2 K L O F ....
3 P I P H O H ....
4 Z A Z J ....
5 A R O P E ....
6 G E R A G E ....
7 C O R K ....

2 Match the music collocations.

1	live	**a**	the charts
2	in	**b**	the world
3	concert	**c**	venue
4	massive	**d**	fans
5	go	**e**	hit
6	release	**f**	music
7	tour	**g**	singer
8	devoted	**h**	performance
9	lead	**i**	solo
10	give	**j**	talent
11	musical	**k**	an album
12	background	**l**	a performance

1 .... 2 .... 3 .... 4 .... 5 .... 6 ....
7 .... 8 .... 9 .... 10 .... 11 .... 12 ....

3 Complete the sentences with the words in the box.

> background   charts   fans   gave
> hit   live   musical   released
> singer   solo   toured   venue

1 I prefer .... performances to listening to music through my headphones.
2 Their first single was a massive .... all over the world.
3 Thousands of devoted .... were waiting outside the stadium.
4 You've got a great voice. Do you want to be the lead .... in my band?
5 I could never play an instrument because I have no .... talent.
6 They're a successful band who have had several singles in the ....
7 We .... our first album online last year, but not many people downloaded it.
8 Lady Gaga .... the world in 2014.
9 She .... a great performance in London.
10 A football stadium is a great choice of concert .... for popular artists.
11 The band split up and the members all went .... in 2012.
12 You can still hear their songs everywhere, from TV ads to .... music in lifts.

READING

1 Have you ever thought about being in a band? Make a list of what steps are necessary to form a band.

....
....
....
....

2 Read the article on page 9. Does it mention any of your steps?

3 Write the questions in the correct place in the text.

1 where's the best place to practise?
2 what are the chances of success?
3 what's the best way to promote a new band?
4 what about putting together a demo?
5 how do you choose your band members?
6 what sort of music should we choose?
7 how do you write songs?

Teen MUSIC SCENE
Interview of the month

We've got a fantastic interview for you this month in *Teen Music Scene*. A lot of you are interested in getting started in the music business, so we've talked to the one-and-only Ricky McKenzie, who set up his band, Ricky's Rockers, when he was 17 – and you all know how successful he is!

TMS: Ricky, welcome. Let's get straight to our readers' questions. First one, A ....?

Ricky: For me, that was the easy part! I was at college with a great bunch of musicians. But there are all sorts of ways to find members – it isn't hard as a lot of people want to be in a band. You can place ads in local colleges, music shops maybe, or even the local press. Or just ask around, you know, friends of friends. Do make it clear which musicians you're looking for though, guitarist, lead singer, so that you don't waste people's time.

TMS: Great ideas! What about the music itself, I mean, B ....?

Ricky: Well, it's important to play what you love! Think of your favourite bands and their styles. You might want to do something a bit different, so mix and match – try mixing styles and find one you all agree on, which can become your own.

TMS: I've got an interesting question here – C ....?

Ricky: That's the hard bit! Not everyone has the musical talent for this, but one or more band members might have. Get the other members to suggest ideas. Maybe one of you has a tune they created. You can all use this as a base to build on. Keep it simple. You'll get there eventually.

TMS: So, you've found your band members, your style, and have written a couple of songs, now D ....?

Ricky: It's important to make sure there's enough space for the band, and that it's somewhere where the noise won't bother other people too much. A garage can be a good place – as long as there isn't a car in it! Some towns and villages have community rooms that you can use either free of charge or at a very low cost.

TMS: Good idea. Now, once you're set up, E ....?

Ricky: Set up your own website and ensure you have a band profile on relevant music websites, with a taste of your music. You could sell some promotional stuff – t-shirts, that kind of thing. You're likely to make more money doing that than from playing live and selling CDs at the beginning!

TMS: Mmm. Regarding CDs, F ....?

Ricky: You must do that, and use a studio to make sure you get a good recording – no bedrooms! Get your songs as near-perfect as possible before recording, as studios are expensive. Three or four songs should be OK.

TMS: Good advice, Ricky. Finally, probably the most frequent question we get – G ....?

Ricky: Well, you have to work hard, practise, keep writing new songs. Make yourselves known: play at local venues and get to know other bands in your area – all contacts are good contacts. And think about an album sooner rather than later. There's a lot of luck involved, but if all goes well, the sky's the limit!

TMS: As you know! Thank you so much, Ricky, it's been great.

4 **Read the article again. Are these statements true (T) or false (F)? Underline the parts of the text which tell you the answer. Then correct the false ones.**

1 It is difficult to find people to play in your band. ....
....

2 It's OK to be influenced by other bands' styles. ....
....

3 You should work together to create songs. ....
....

4 You may have to pay for a room to practise in. ....
....

5 The best way to make money is to sell CDs and play concerts. ....
....

6 It's good to use studio time to practise your songs. ....

7 Make friends with people doing the same sort of thing as you. ....
....

EP Word profile *on*

Match the phrases with the definitions, then use the phrases to complete the sentences.

1 only if
2 available
3 generally
4 not early or late
5 intentionally
6 because of

a on offer
b on the whole
c on time
d on condition that
e on account of
f on purpose

1 ...... 2 ...... 3 ...... 4 ...... 5 ...... 6 ......

1 You must arrive .... for your appointment at the recording studio.

2 The band had some CDs .... at their concert.

3 ...., I think their latest album was very good.

4 I'll join your band .... I can choose the name.

5 .... the fact that the guitarist had a broken finger, the concert was cancelled.

6 Did you do that .... or was it an accident?

GRAMMAR Present tenses

1 Choose the correct answer.

1 **A:** What's the name of that song you *play /*
   're playing now? It *sounds / 's sounding* great!

   B: It's called 'Three little birds'. *Do you want /*
   Are you wanting me to teach it to you?

2 **A:** Where is Dana? I *don't see / haven't seen* her
   for hours.

   B: She *runs / 's running* in the park. She always
   goes / is going for a run on Sundays.

   A: I should do something like that. Running
   keeps / is keeping you fit.

3 **A:** *Do you go / Are you going* to the concert at the
   Rialto tonight?

   B: I *don't know / 'm not knowing.* Who *plays /*
   's playing?

   A: The Creds. They *are touring / have toured* the
   country since May.

   B: Mmm, I *don't like / 'm not liking* The Creds.

4 **A:** *Have you still sung / Are you still singing* in that
   band?

   B: What, the one at school? Yes, I *'m / 've been*
   with them for nearly a year now.

   A: *Have you done / Do you do* any concerts
   recently?

   B: Yes, quite a few. In fact, we *give / 're giving* one
   tomorrow evening. Why don't you come?

**2 Write sentences from the words. Use the correct
present tense.**

0 I / go / to a concert / this weekend
   ....*I'm going to a concert this weekend*...........

1 He / always / have / a burger before / he / play

   ....
   ....

2 Donna / seem / enjoy / dancing

   ....
   ....

3 You / obviously / do / lots of exercise nowadays.

   ....
   ....

4 I / love / this band / since before they were famous

   ....
   ....

5 You / need / practise / to be any good

   ....
   ....

6 Kerry / not / understand / why / her friends / love /
   hip-hop.

   ....
   ....

7 Pablo / learn / how to play / the piano / at the
   moment.

   ....

8 Marcin and his band / write / several new songs /
   since their last concert.

   ....
   ....

**3 Complete the email with the verbs in brackets in
the correct present tense.**

> Hi guys
> I ¹ .... (think) about booking
> a couple of hours at the recording studio
> next week so we can make our demo. I
> ² .... (need) to know what day
> and time everyone can make it. We all
> ³ .... (go) to school every day, so
> it ⁴ .... (have to) be an evening
> or Saturday. Danny ⁵ .... (have)
> driving lessons every Monday and Wednesday
> night, and I ⁶ .... (do) karate
> on Tuesdays and Thursdays – so that leaves
> Friday or Saturday.
> Sue, ⁷ .... (you / go) to Jake's
> party on Friday? If not, let's try for that day.
> The studio ⁸ .... (cost) €80 an
> hour, but that's OK. We ⁹ .... (be)
> together as a band for six months now, and I
> ¹⁰ .... (think) we're ready.
> Got to go now – Mum ¹¹ ....
> (cook) dinner and ¹² .... (want)
> me to lay the table. Call me!
> Steve

**4 ⊙ Correct the mistakes in these sentences or
put a tick (✔) by any you think are correct.**

1 The older dancers are teaching our traditional
   dance classes every week. ....

2 I am writing to complain about your report
   concerning the music festival. ....

3 Like everyone, I had some embarrassing
   moments in my life. ....

4 In both restaurants they play calm,
   melodious music, which creates a
   nice atmosphere. ....

5 They're very popular and they're playing
   very good music. ....

6 I have very broad experience of organising
   summer camps because I am working in
   summer camps for foreign school children
   for about ten years. ....

VOCABULARY Verbs + infinitive / -ing with a change in meaning

1 Match the sentences to their meanings in each pair.

1 I tried running, but I soon got bored.
2 I tried to run, but my coat was trapped in the door.

a it was difficult
b it was an experiment

3 We stopped to get something to eat.
4 We stopped eating and got in the car.

a it was the reason we stopped
b the activity stopped

5 He remembered locking the door.
6 He remembered to lock the door.

a he didn't forget to do the action
b he recalled the action

7 I forgot to go to the internet café.
8 I'll never forget going to an internet café for the first time.

a I will remember the experience
b I didn't remember to do the action

2 Complete the sentences with the correct form of the words in the box.

> lock   reach   talk   turn   watch   win

1 Jake forgot .... his bike when he went into the shop, and it was gone when he came out.
2 My aunt Becky is lovely but she's quite tiring to be with because she never stops .... !
3 'I can't get this TV to work.' 'Have you tried .... it off and on again?'
4 I'll always remember .... the world championship in 1995.
5 Lucy was trying .... the biscuits at the top of the cupboard when she fell off the chair.
6 We were driving home but it was such a beautiful evening that we stopped .... the sunset.

LISTENING

1 You will hear four people talking about their experience of a music festival. Tick (✔) the topics you think they will talk about.

1 the music ☐
2 camping at the festival ☐
3 the food ☐
4 the weather ☐
5 safety ☐
6 comedy acts ☐
7 prices ☐
8 staff at the festival ☐
9 parking ☐
10 communications ☐

2 ▶2 Listen to the four people and check your answers to exercise 1.

3 Read the questions. Match the underlined words to the phrases with a similar meaning below.

A appreciates the <u>variety of bands</u> performing   ....
B enjoys having a <u>wide choice of places to eat</u>   ....
C <u>regularly</u> goes to events like this   ....
D is happy about how easy it is to <u>find your way around</u>   ....
E is pleasantly surprised by the <u>quality of the facilities</u>   ....
F is disappointed at <u>how expensive things are</u>   ....

1 I've been doing it for years.
2 The campsite provides excellent accommodation.
3 Everyone's taste in music is covered.
4 There's food from every corner of the world.
5 You can't get lost.
6 Nothing's cheap.

4 ▶2 Listen again. Choose from the list A–F the main point each speaker makes about the festivals they've been to. There are two extra letters which you do not need.

Speaker 1 ....   Speaker 3 ....
Speaker 2 ....   Speaker 4 ....

VOCABULARY Verbs of communication

1 Complete the crossword, using the clues below.

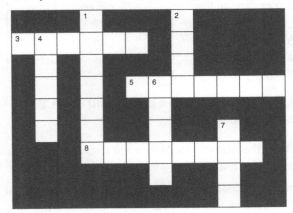

Across

3 Don't … me of being lazy. I'm just really tired today.

5 Donna will never … to doing anything wrong.

8 Did the teacher … to keep everyone in after class? He often does that.

Down

1 I … you spend more time studying and less time playing games.

2 I forgot to … you not to leave your bike outside.

4 Steven didn't … to be an expert – he just said he'd played the game before.

6 I'm not going to … you to do anything – you only have to do it if you want to.

7 It's obvious that you didn't enjoy my story, so don't try to … it.

2 Choose the correct answers.

1 I completely *deny / confess / accuse* dropping your laptop.

2 Conor *threatened / suggested / claimed* that they all go to the cinema.

3 I'm *ordering / denying / warning* you – it's dangerous to walk through the park at night.

4 My mum *threatened / accused / suggested* to sell the X-box if we didn't help her with the housework.

5 You have been *warned / denied / accused* of a very serious crime.

6 OK, OK, I *deny / confess / order* that I didn't go to school this morning.

7 The teacher *threatened / ordered / suggested* the whole class to stay behind after school.

8 Are you *claiming / warning / accusing* that the dog ate your homework?

3 Rewrite the sentences using one of the verbs from exercises 1 and 2.

> I'll stop your pocket money if you don't tidy your room.

0 Dad ....*threatened to stop my pocket money.*......

> No, I did not eat the last piece of cake!

1 Sara ....
....

> You broke the window, didn't you, Gary?

2 Mum ....
....

> Don't play football in the street, kids – it's dangerous.

3 The police officer ....
....

> Why don't we download that new comedy film?

4 Mike ....
....

READING

1 Can you think of any famous brothers and sisters, either modern-day or from history?

....
....

2 Quickly read the four short biographies and match them to the photos.

Famous brothers and sisters

The Brontës

Picture ....

In the mid-19th century, three English sisters, Emily, Charlotte and Anne, made a huge impression on the literary world. When they were children, the three girls, and their brother Branwell, used to create fictional worlds together. They were inspired by twelve wooden soldiers which their father had given them. Their first stories were written in tiny books of about 4 x 6.5 cm in size – just right for the little soldiers to read.

They continued to write poems and stories into adulthood. Then, in 1847, all three sisters had novels published – and they were a great success. As it was considered very unusual for women to publish books in those days, they all used men's names. In fact, some readers at the time believed the novels were all the work of one man!

Haim

Picture ....

The three sisters Alana, Danielle and Este Haim grew up in California. They got their love of music from their parents and spent much of their childhood listening to the classic rock records from the 1970s which they owned. Their musical careers started while they were still at school, when their parents formed a 'family band'. They used to play at charity fairs and they never made much money.

In 2006 the girls decided to form their own band. They played at local venues but because all three sisters were doing other things, they did not take the band too seriously. After Este graduated in 2010, Danielle finished high school and Alana left college they released three songs as a free download on their website. Since then, they have become one of America's most successful pop bands.

The Wright brothers

Picture ....

Wilbur and Orville Wright are brothers famous for inventing the first aeroplane. Their interest in flight started on the day their father brought home a toy helicopter for them. It was made of paper and wood, and was made to work with a rubber band. The boys played with it until it broke, and then made their own to replace it.

When they were older, they owned a bicycle shop where they started manufacturing and selling their own bikes. This provided them with the money to pay for their experiments in flight. Eventually, they built their 'flying machine'. Although it worked very well, it took several years before any government or business took them seriously enough to give them any money!

The Williams sisters

Picture ....

When you think of famous sporting sisters, the first names to spring to mind are Venus and Serena. The Williams sisters grew up in a poor area of Los Angeles, where their father Richard taught them to play tennis. When she was only ten years old, Venus – the older of the two – could serve the ball at speeds of over 160 kph!

The sisters entered the professional tennis circuit in their early teens, and soon began to dominate the game. Between them they have won dozens of titles – often playing against each other in the finals. But, in spite of their competitive natures, they remain very close. In fact, they share a house in Florida.

---

3 **According to the texts, which of the brothers/ sisters did the following?**

1 were influenced by their parents' tastes

....

2 were inspired by a childhood gift

....

3 won prizes

....

4 caused disbelief

....

5 were successful before they became adults

....

6 worked together to produce something artistic

....

EP **Word profile** *once*

Complete the sentences with the words and phrases in the box.

> at once   for once   once   once
> once again   once in a while

1 I'm glad you have arrived on time

....

2 .... I know where I'm staying, I'll email you with my address.

3 She likes to go for a swim in the river

....

4 Go and tidy your room ....

5 I will tell you ...., but that will be the third and last time.

6 I .... believed that I would be famous one day, but I don't any more.

GRAMMAR Past tenses

1 Choose the correct answer.

1 When I *was / had been* a little girl, I *was getting / used to get* really excited about getting on a bus. Then I *started / had started* school and I *had / was having* to take the bus every day. It's not so exciting any more.

2 We *didn't have / weren't having* much money this time last year. My dad *worked / had worked* in a shoe factory and my mum *was being / was* a waitress. Then, in January this year, we *watched / were watching* TV in the living room when Dad *came / had come* home and *was telling / told* us he *was winning / had won* six million euros!

3 **A:** What *had you done / were you doing* at 10 o'clock last night?
   B: I *slept / was sleeping*. It *had been / was being* a long, hard day.

2 Match the beginnings and endings of the sentences.

1 Once I had finished my homework, ...
2 I was walking home from school ....
3 I used to watch a lot of Disney movies ....
4 I picked up my mobile phone ....
5 When I was a little baby, ...
6 I hadn't heard the door bell ....

a and texted my friend Rachel.
b my mother used to sing to me.
c when I saw the bus crash into the wall.
d I went to the park to play football.
e but I don't now.
f so I was surprised to find a parcel on the floor outside.

3 Complete the text with the verbs in the box in the correct form.

be   break   enjoy   fill   finish
forget   jump   laugh   lie   walk

When we ¹ .... kids, my brother and I ² .... playing tricks on each other. Making my brother jump in fright was my favourite trick. I ³ .... for ages when I did that! One sunny day, my brother ⁴ .... in the garden, on the grass, just near the back door, which was made of glass. We ⁵ .... just .... school for the day, so it was about 3.30 in the afternoon. I went to the kitchen and ⁶ .... a large cup full of water. Then I ⁷ .... quietly towards the garden, on my toes, intending to jump through the door and surprise him with a face full of water. Instead, I ⁸ .... straight into the back door, and ⁹ .... my nose on the hard glass. I ¹⁰ .... to open the door!

4 ⊙ Correct the mistakes in these sentences or put a tick (✔) by any you think are correct.

1 I remember the times we were going to the sea.
   ....

2 I was lying in my bed while it was raining outside which I hated, especially in the morning. ....

3 He saw that the door is broken. ....

4 When we went to the beach, we use to swim all day. ....

5 I had visited it last weekend and I greatly enjoyed the festival. ....

VOCABULARY Phrasal verbs: relationships

1 Complete the sentences with the correct form of the phrasal verbs in the box.

back up   fall out   go through
identify with   laugh at   pick on

1 I find it hard to .... rich pop stars, because their lives are so different from mine.

2 I'm worried that everyone will .... my new hairstyle.

3 You shouldn't .... someone because of the way they look – it's cruel and unfair.

4 My friendship with the girl next door .... a tough time when she ignored me at a party.

5 My best friend and I .... for a while, but we are friends again now.

6 Nobody believed my story, and none of my friends .... me ....

2 Rewrite the sentences, using the verbs from exercise 1.

1 They had an argument and aren't talking.
   ....
   ....

2 He felt that he understood and shared the feelings of his older brother.
   ....
   ....

3 We've experienced a difficult period in our friendship.
   ....
   ....

4 You shouldn't criticise Adam unfairly.
   ....
   ....

5 I'm worried that I will amuse everyone with my stupidity.
   ....
   ....

6 Why didn't you support her?
   ....
   ....

WRITING Apologies

See Prepare to write box, Student's Book page 23.

1 Match the apologies to the responses.

❶

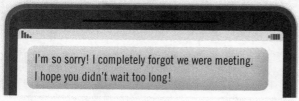

Sorry! There was only one yoghurt left and I was so hungry I ate it, even though I knew it was yours.

❷

I'm so sorry! I completely forgot we were meeting. I hope you didn't wait too long!

❸

Dear Mr Smith
Please accept our apologies for the poor service you received at our café on Monday afternoon. The waiter was new to the job and had clearly not been give adequate training. We would like to offer you a free meal for two the next time

Ⓐ

Dear Mrs Jones
Thank you for your offer. My friend and I will certainly visit again sometime next week. I just hope

Ⓑ

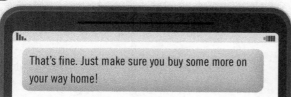

That's fine. Just make sure you buy some more on your way home!

Ⓒ

Hi John
It's not the first time this has happened but believe me, it's the last! You're so unreliable! Please don't call, text or email me again.

1 .... 2 .... 3 ....

2 The paragraphs in this email are out of order. Read the email quickly. What is Martin apologising for?

....

....

Martin Briant
Sent: 02 July 2015
To: Angela Smith

Dear Mrs Smith

A
Once again, I'm really sorry, Mrs Smith. I'm going to ride only in the skate park from now on! See you tomorrow.

B
It happened because I was going much too fast around the corner, and I wasn't concentrating properly. I am usually a good skateboarder and I don't like to take risks. I don't know what I was thinking about that day!

C
I'm writing to apologise for crashing into you when I was riding my skateboard the other day. It was my fault entirely.

D
I hope you are not hurt. You very kindly said you were all right and that I shouldn't worry, but I still feel terrible about it. Is there anything I can do to help you? Maybe I could tidy your garden or something. Let me know what you'd like me to do, and I'll do it.

Best wishes,
Martin

3 Number the paragraphs in the correct order.

1 .... 2 .... 3 .... 4 ....

4 Now match each paragraph to these functions.

an apology for what happened ....
an offer to improve the situation ....
a final apology ....
the reasons for what happened ....

5 You borrowed a DVD from a friend and lost it. Write an email apologising to your friend, following the paragraph structure in exercises 2 to 4.

④ Forces of nature

VOCABULARY   Natural disasters: verbs

1 Match the verbs in the box to the pictures.

| collapse | crack | drag | erupt | float | knock over | run | shake | smash |

a ....   b ....   c ....   d ....   e ....

f ....   g ....   h ....   i ....

2 Write sentences describing the pictures, using the verbs in exercise 1.

0 building .....*The building is shaking.*.....................................

1 ground ....

2 volcano ....

3 lava / side ....

....

4 car / lamppost ....

....

5 man / sofa ....

....

3 Complete the sentences with the correct form of the verbs in exercise 1.

1 The suitcase was too heavy to lift, so I .... it to the car.

2 Our kitchen was flooded because someone had left the tap ....

3 The city of Pompeii was destroyed when a volcano .... in 79 CE.

4 A hot-air balloon .... over our house this morning.

5 The window .... when the stone hit it, but it did not break completely.

6 Every time a train went past our tent, the ground ....

7 He was so heavy that the chair .... under his weight.

8 I wasn't looking where I was going and I accidentally .... an old lady.

9 She .... the bottle by throwing it against the wall.

READING

1 Look at the definition of *tornado* and read the text on page 17 quickly. What two unusual things does it mention that tornadoes can do?

....

....

> **tornado (n):** an extremely strong and dangerous wind that blows in a circle and destroys buildings as it moves along

2 The topic sentences below are missing from the paragraphs in the text. Match them to the correct paragraph.

1 Known as 'fire tornadoes', they usually occur when a large wildfire is in progress.

2 However, it seems that fish are the most common thing to fall from the clouds (apart from rain).

3 Nobody really says it any more, but you've probably heard the old-fashioned English expression 'it's raining cats and dogs' to describe very heavy rain.

4 The phenomenon is quite easy to explain.

5 Glen Mason is one man who saw a fire tornado close up.

6 These stories tend to make light of the true nature of tornadoes, though.

A

.... The origin of this idiom is unknown, and it has almost certainly never happened in real life. However, many other surprising things have been known to fall from the sky, such as fish and frogs: one morning in May, 1981, the citizens of Naphlion, a city in southern Greece, were surprised to wake up to find small green frogs falling from the sky. They landed in trees, on roofs and on the streets. The species of frog came from North Africa, hundreds of kilometres away!

B

.... Small whirlwinds or tornadoes may form in certain weather conditions, which can pick up small things – creatures or objects – when they pass over water. These can then be carried for many kilometres, and eventually, they will be dropped by the clouds carrying them. This results in the shower of fish, frogs or whatever the winds have picked up. There have been reports of tomatoes, and even rocks, being dropped from the sky.

C

.... They are the lightest and most common inhabitants of water, after all. In one town in Honduras, a 'Rain of Fish' happens every year. The people of the area even have a festival to celebrate the occasion.

D

.... They are a force of nature that can be truly terrifying. There are many types of tornado and while most are relatively harmless, like the ones described above, every year parts of the world experience huge tornadoes, which can bring extreme destruction. They have been known to destroy whole towns, and kill thousands of people. And worse, some of them can be made of fire.

E

.... These fires are so hot that they can create their own wind, which can turn into a spinning whirlwind of flame. Under the right conditions, they can grow to over 10 metres wide and 300 metres tall. Although fire tornadoes usually move quite slowly, they can cause an incredible amount of destruction. They will set anything in their way on fire and throw burning objects into the surrounding areas. Sometimes they can last for more than an hour, and it is impossible to put them out. You just have to wait.

F

.... He watched it for over half an hour before it finally died. 'It was about 500 metres away and it sounded just like a jet plane,' he said. 'It was terrifying, but also the most amazing and exciting thing I've ever seen. I'm a very lucky man – both to have seen it and to have survived it!'

3 **Read the text again. Are these statements about the text true or false? Write T or F, and correct the false ones.**

1 It is not known where the phrase 'raining cats and dogs' comes from. ....

....

2 In Naphlion, people were surprised to see rocks falling from the sky. ....

....

3 Objects are picked up from the water by clouds. ....

....

4 In certain parts of the world, fish fall from the sky regularly. ....

....

5 Fire tornadoes are not so dangerous when they move slowly.

....

6 Glen Mason is glad that he experienced a fire tornado. ....

EP **Word profile** *term*

Match the phrases with *term* to their meanings.

1 In the short term, we have to make sure that everybody knows what their job is. ....

2 In ecological terms, the new factory will be a disaster. ....

3 We need to think about how to proceed in the long term. ....

4 In terms of energy use, we could make a lot of savings. ....

5 The term 'eco-friendly' is used for things which do not harm the environment. ....

6 You can't do that because it goes against the terms of your contract. ....

a regarding, or in relation to

b over a period of time that only continues for a short way into the future

c explaining which part of a problem or situation you are referring to

d over a period of time that continues a long way into the future

e the rules of an agreement

f a word or phrase meaning a particular thing

GRAMMAR   Making comparisons

1 **Choose the correct answer.**

1 That is .... the most amazing thing I have ever seen.
   a slightly   **b** easily   **c** far

2 My computer is a .... deal faster than yours.
   a quite   **b** good   **c** big

3 Volcanoes are .... more terrifying than thunderstorms.
   a good   **b** quite   **c** far

4 My little sister is .... as tall as me.
   a slightly   **b** almost   **c** a good deal

5 This medicine has made me feel .... worse.
   a easily   **b** not quite   **c** a good deal

6 The more you practise, ... you will become.
   a the best   **b** the better   **c** the good

7 Can I have a .... larger piece of cake, please?
   a slightly   **b** easily   **c** quite

8 My grade was not .... as good as I expected.
   a almost   **b** easily   **c** quite

2 **Complete the sentences with the adjective pairs in brackets. Use the ... the ... .**

0 .....The larger..... asteroids are, ...the easier..... they are to see. (large / easy)

1 My grandfather says .... you get, ... it becomes to change. (old / hard)

2 .... the weather, ... my sister is. (hot / happy)

3 .... you are, ... it is to ride your bike. (sleepy / dangerous)

4 .... it got, ... it became. (late / dark)

5 .... you wait, ... it will become to do anything. (long / difficult)

3 **Complete the second sentence so that it means the same as the first.**

0 That's the scariest film I've ever seen, by far. (easily)
   That's ..easily the scariest film.. I've ever seen.

1 A rhinoceros is not quite as big as an elephant. (slightly)
   An elephant .... rhinoceros.

2 Tonya is not quite as clever as Kaye. (almost)
   Tonya .... as Kaye.

3 That party was much more interesting than I expected. (a good deal)
   That party .... than I expected.

4 You'll need to study a good deal harder if you want to succeed. (far)
   You'll need to .... if you want to succeed.

5 Mr Andrews is much stricter than Ms Knight. (a lot less)
   Ms Knight is .... than Mr Andrews.

4 👁 **Choose the correct sentence in each pair.**

1 **a** It was far better from all the other songs that I had heard.
  b It was far better than all the other songs that I had heard.

2 **a** The hotel is much more cheaper, and they have good bar food.
  b The hotel is much cheaper, and they have good bar food.

3 **a** As much as you study, as much as you will improve your English.
  b The more you study, the more you will improve your English.

4 **a** I hope to see many more films next year.
  b I hope to see much more films next year.

VOCABULARY   too, so, such

1 **Choose the correct answers.**

1 It was so / too hot outside that you could fry an egg on the pavement.

2 Sophia has so / such a beautiful voice!

3 It's much so / too risky to swim in this river.

4 There are so / such many things to see in this city.

5 This coffee is far too / such cold to drink – I'm sending it back.

6 It was so / such a funny film that my sides hurt by the end of it.

7 That restaurant is far so / too expensive to eat in every week.

8 I'm so / such happy I could dance!

2 **Rewrite the sentences with too, so or such.**

0 You have such lovely eyes! (so)
   ....Your eyes are so lovely!............................

1 The book was too boring to finish. (such)
   ....
   ....

2 The exam was so hard that nobody got a good mark. (too)
   ....
   ....

3 She's such a kind person that everyone loves her. (so)
   ....
   ....

4 My dog eats too much food for me to afford to keep it. (so)
   ....
   ....

5 The holiday apartment we stayed in was so quiet that you could hear the insects. (such)
   ....
   ....

LISTENING

1 Label the pictures with the words in the box.

> earthquake   flood   volcano   wildfire

a ....
b ....
c ....
d ....

2 ▶3 Listen to parts of four news reports. Match the topic of each news report to the pictures in exercise 1.

1 ......   2 ....   3 ....   4 ....

3 ▶3 Listen again and complete the journalists' notes with numbers, dates or one or two words.

1
Time of earthquake: [1] ....
Length of earthquake: [2] ....
seconds
Year of previous big earthquake:
[3] ....

2
Large volcanic [4] ....
on island of Morania
People trying to escape [5] ....
running down mountain
Danger of complete [6] ....

3
This is the [7] .... time this has
happened recently.
Water [8] ....through the
streets of Bigham
People angry at [9] ....

4
Number of homes destroyed:
over [10] ....
Firefighting made difficult by
[11] ....
Number of injured: [12] ....

---

4 Answer the questions.

1 In 1, why are people afraid to return to their houses?

....

2 In 2, how are people escaping from the island?

....

3 In 3, why are people in the village of Bigham angry?

....

4 In 4, what do people think caused the disaster?

....

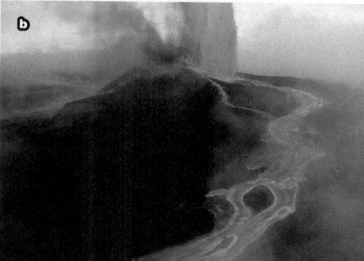

5 Virtual action

VOCABULARY   Video games: verbs

1 Complete the crossword, using the clues below.

Across
2 control the direction of a vehicle
6 run after someone or something in order to catch them
8 work together with someone in order to achieve the same aim
10 drive a vehicle backwards
11 move on your hands and knees

Down
1 build something from several parts
3 give something to someone and receive something similar from them
4 be in a position where you will not fall to either side, or put something in this position
5 go past a vehicle or person that is going in the same direction
7 collect several things, often from different places or people
9 make a vehicle move more slowly or stop
10 move somewhere by turning in a circular direction

2 Choose the correct answers.

1 Let's go out and *chase / gather* some flowers from the garden.
2 This bike is so heavy that it is hard to *steer / brake* in the right direction.
3 I *balanced / crawled* under the bed to look for my mobile.
4 You have to *construct / cooperate* a city in this game.
5 How long can you *balance / roll* on one foot for?
6 An angry dog *chased / braked* me on the way home last night.
7 We'll never finish this project if we don't *cooperate / exchange.*
8 Do you want to *balance / exchange* this computer for a bicycle?
9 The Ferrari's going too slowly – why doesn't he *overtake / reverse* it?
10 When I fell off my skateboard, it *rolled / chased* to the bottom of the hill without me.
11 She'll never drive forwards into that parking space – she'll have to *crawl / reverse.*
12 If he doesn't *brake / gather* soon, he'll crash on the next corner.

EP Word profile *catch*

Match the uses of *catch* to their meanings.

1 You have to try to catch all of the animals in this game. ....
2 I missed school, and now I have to catch up on what we've been doing. ....
3 Quick, that red car is catching us up! ....
4 He caught the glass as it fell from the table. ....
5 You'll catch a cold if you go out in this weather! ....
6 What train are you catching tomorrow? ....
7 My mum caught me playing video games instead of doing my homework. ....
8 The Lamborghini crashed into a wall and caught fire. ....
9 Something in the window caught my attention. ....
10 I hope they catch the thief soon. ....
11 Did you catch up with your old friend from primary school last weekend? ....

a find and stop someone or something escaping
b reach someone or something in front of you by going faster than them
c do something that you weren't able to do earlier
d meet someone you know after a long time and talk about what you have been doing
e find and take away a criminal
f make someone notice something and feel interested
g get an illness, especially one you get from another person
h start burning
i discover someone doing something wrong or something secret
j take hold of something, especially something moving through the air
k get on a bus, train, etc. in order to travel somewhere

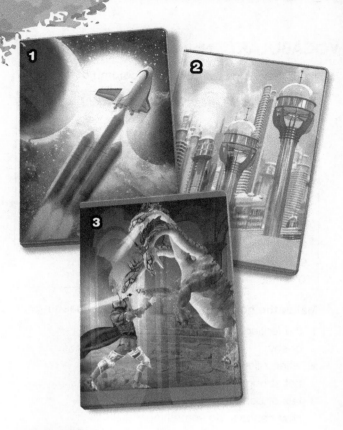

READING

1 Look at the covers of the three video games. Which do you think would be the most fun to play? ....

2 You are going to read a review of the three video games in exercise 1. Write down two or three words that you might find in each one.

A ....

B ....

C ....

3 Read the video game reviews and match them to the correct picture. Check your answers to exercise 2.

4 Choose the game to answer the question. Sometimes more than one answer is possible. Underline the sections which give you the answers.

Which game

	A	B	C
1 gets the best review?	....	....	....
2 gets the worst review?	....	....	....
3 does not have good music?	....	....	....
4 has the best graphics?	....	....	....
5 has the worst graphics?	....	....	....
6 is educational?	....	....	....
7 involves fighting?	....	....	....
8 is surprisingly difficult?	....	....	....
9 is the least difficult?	....	....	....
10 has no original ideas?	....	....	....

JIMMY'S GAME REVIEWS

A ROCKET RACE (picture ....)

Rocket Race is the latest game from the highly successful SpeedCo games producer. They have produced every racing game imaginable, from racing cars to horses – but this is the first time they have left planet Earth!

As you can probably guess, it's all about racing rockets – and it's great fun! You have full control over the design of your vehicle, which you then construct and race against a team of other pilots. There is a choice of over twenty different race routes that take you round spectacular planets, asteroids and other parts of the universe. The graphics are truly superb.

The only criticism I have of the game is the music. I don't know who decided a rock soundtrack was a good idea, but it's not what I would choose. I think it sounds dreadful!

But overall, it's a really good game – especially for children as it's quite easy – and I'd certainly recommend it to anyone who enjoys racing games and outer space.

B MEN AND MONSTERS (picture ....)

You might think that the games market doesn't need another fantasy role-playing game, but Middle Earth Games have other ideas. This game sends you to find the magic Ring of Argor. You'll have endless adventures on the way, avoiding traps, picking up friends and weapons, and of course battling monsters.

There are ten levels to complete and as you go through them, you become more and more powerful. This is good, because the levels get more and more difficult to finish. It's challenging, but that's what you'd expect from this producer of intelligent games.

I do think that the graphics could be improved though. They looked a bit old-fashioned to me, which made the game less enjoyable. The accompanying music wasn't so great, either.

This is really a game for fans of fantasy role plays. To an experienced gamer, it doesn't really offer anything new. It's OK as far as it goes, but it doesn't go very far.

C NATION BUILDER (picture ....)

Have you ever wanted to be the ruler of your own country? With *Nation Builder*, the latest release from DespotGamesUK, you can. But watch out – it's not as easy as it looks!

You start with nothing – just a field in the middle of nowhere – and build from there. Gathering building materials is your first job, as you have to make a house of some kind before night, when your enemies come out. If you can't protect yourself from them, you have to start again. The longer you survive, the more people come to live with you and cooperate with you in the war against your enemies. Eventually you have your own nation.

I can't think of anything bad to say about this game! It's packed with great features: the graphics are good, the way you build your nation is really clever, and the possibilities are only limited by your own imagination. Not only is it great fun, but you learn a lot about the day-to-day running of a country.

Seriously, I can't recommend this game highly enough. Buy it!

GRAMMAR Relative clauses

1 Complete the sentences with *who, which* or *where*.

1 This is the computer game ....
   my parents gave me for my birthday.
2 Is this the shop .... you usually buy
   your lunch?
3 My uncle, ... works in the gaming
   industry, is a very rich man.
4 Sondra is the girl .... invited me to
   your party.
5 I don't understand people .... don't
   enjoy sports.
6 Last year we went to California, ...
   a lot of computer software is designed.
7 What's the address of the games review website
   .... you were telling me about?
8 The girl .... won the competition was
   only 13 years old.
9 *Minecraft* is a game .... is really good
   fun to play.
10 I prefer to play games in my room,
   .... I'm not likely to be disturbed.

2 Which of the sentences in exercise 1 contain
pronouns which can be replaced by *that*?

....

3 Choose the correct answers and put the commas
in the correct place.

0 My brother, (who) / *which* is two years older than
  me, doesn't like games.
1 I played for five hours yesterday *that / which* is
  much too long.
2 Hollywood *which / where* the American film
  industry is based is an expensive place to live.
3 John *that / who* lives next door to me has a huge
  collection of games.
4 This is my friend Stella *who / that* goes to the same
  school as me.
5 The game takes place in a city called Titania
  which / that is attacked by aliens.
6 The games shop in the mall *which / where*
  my cousin Max works has a sale this week.

4 ⊙ Correct the mistakes in these sentences or
put a tick (✔) by any you think are correct.

1 I suggest we visit the National History Museum,
  wich I have never seen before. ....
2 Thanks for your letter, which I received last week.
  ....
3 He had a best friend, that was more like a brother
  to him. ....
4 I would help in preparing the things that would
  be necessary. ....
5 It was nice for those attended. ....

VOCABULARY Nouns: *-ness* and *-ment*

1 Write the nouns in the correct column of the table.

	-ness	-ment
1 argue		
2 arrange		
3 dark		
4 embarrass		
5 encourage		
6 fit		
7 friendly		
8 great		
9 treat		
10 weak		

2 Match the nouns in exercise 1 to their meanings.

1 the feeling of being ashamed
  or shy   ....
2 when someone or something is
  not strong   ....
3 talk or behaviour that gives you
  confidence to do something   ....
4 an angry discussion with someone
  in which you disagree   ....
5 the quality of behaving in a kind,
  pleasant way to someone   ....
6 the condition of being physically
  strong and healthy   ....
7 skill and importance   ....
8 when there is little or no light   ....
9 the way you deal with or behave
  towards someone or something   ....
10 plan for how something will
  happen   ....

3 Complete the sentences with some of the nouns
from exercises 1 and 2.

1 He won't do it on his own – he needs some
  ....
2 I know the owner of this café, which is why I get
  special ....
3 When I fell off my bike, my ....
  meant I couldn't ask for help.
4 We were all made very happy by the
  .... of the hotel staff.
5 The storm caused an electrical failure and the
  whole house was in complete ....
  for hours.
6 They haven't spoken to each other since they
  had that terrible .... about computer
  games.
7 He'll need to improve his .... if he
  wants to get picked for the athletics team.
8 You will achieve .... only if you have
  talent and you work hard.

WRITING An email (2)

1 **Read the email to Tim. What is its purpose?**

a making a suggestion ☐

b asking for advice ☐

c offering an opinion ☐

> Hi Tim
>
> I'm writing to you because you are an experienced gamer. We're going on a family holiday next week. It's going to be a long journey, so I'm looking for one or two great games to play on my phone while we're travelling. Have you got any suggestions? Somebody recommended *Men and Monsters*. They said it was really good fun. What do you think of it?
>
> Looking forward to hearing from you.
>
> Simon

2 **Read Tim's reply. Does he recommend *Men and Monsters*? What does he say about it?**

....

....

3 **Replace the highlighted phrases with an extreme adjective from the box.**

> ancient   dreadful   fascinating   packed with
> ridiculous   superb

1 ....   4 ....

2 ....   5 ....

3 ....   6 ....

> Hi Simon
>
> Good to hear from you!
>
> *Men and Monsters* got some good reviews online, but I didn't like it much. The graphics looked ¹ very old and the story was ² very silly. The only thing I liked was the music.
>
> I'd recommend *Rocket Race*. That will keep you entertained on the journey. It's about racing rockets, and it's ³ really interesting. The game is ⁴ very full of special effects and quite difficult in places. The best thing about the game is the graphics – they are ⁵ very good! The only thing I didn't like about it was the music. They use too much rock and it's ⁶ really bad.
>
> Anyway, I hope you have a great holiday. Let's catch up when you get back. You can tell me what you thought of the game.
>
> Cheers,
>
> Tim

4 **Look at these parts of Tim's reply. Number them 1–6 in the order they appear in the email.**

a say what you especially like about the game ☐

b say hello ☐

c say what you think of *Men and Monsters* ☐

d wish Simon a happy holiday ☐

e describe the game ☐

f recommend a game ☐

5 **Plan your own reply to Simon. If you don't know a good game, you can use *Nation Builder* from page 21 of this unit. Use the structure in exercise 4 to make notes in the table.**

Part of reply	Notes	Possible adjectives
beginning		
opinion of *Men and Monsters*		
recommendation of game		
description		
good points		
ending		

6 **Write your reply to Simon.**

- Use your notes from exercise 5.
- Use some extreme adjectives in your email.
- Write about 120–150 words.
- Check your spelling and grammar.

6 Creative eating

VOCABULARY Food and drink: phrasal verbs

1 Choose a verb from A and prepositions from B to make phrasal verbs, then write them by their meanings.

A

cut   cut   eat   eat
fill   go   heat   live

B

down on   off   on   out
out   up   up   up

1 .... : become full and unable to eat more
2 .... : eat or drink less of something
3 .... : stop eating or drinking something
4 .... : eat in a restaurant
5 .... : only eat a particular type of food
6 .... : eat all the food you have been given
7 .... : make food hot so it can be eaten
8 .... : stop being good to eat because it is too old

2 Complete the sentences with the phrasal verbs from exercise 1.

1 We don't .... much because restaurants are expensive in this town.
2 My doctor told me to .... the amount of red meat I eat.
3 You can't have any pudding unless you .... everything on your plate, Charlie!
4 I don't want to cook, so I'll just .... something in the microwave.
5 If you haven't had enough at the end of a meal, you can always .... with some fruit.
6 I have .... tea and coffee completely and I'm sleeping much better now.
7 If you don't drink that milk soon, it will ....
8 We more or less .... rice and potatoes at home – it's a bit boring, to be honest.

3 Write sentences, using the words given. Add the correct preposition to each one and put the verb(s) in the correct tense.

0 Mum and Dad / eat / together / once a month.
   ...Mum and Dad eat out together once...
   ...a month.

1 I / heat / some milk / for / hot chocolate / right now.
   ....
   ....

2 This meat / go / It / smell / dreadful.
   ....
   ....

3 You / must / eat / all / your vegetables, Annie!
   ....
   ....

4 No more for me, thanks. / That pie / fill / me!
   ....
   ....

5 My sister / cut / chocolate / from her diet last month.
   ....
   ....

6 Luke's brother / almost / live / meat and potatoes.
   ....
   ....

READING

1 Look at the photos on page 25. Which foods are healthy and which are unhealthy? Add some more to the table.

Healthy	Unhealthy

2 Do you eat healthily? Tick (✔) the advice you follow. Can you think of any other tips for healthy eating?

1 Choose the healthy option. ☐
2 Eat five portions of fruit and vegetables per day. ☐
3 Know what you're eating. ☐
4 Avoid unhealthy snacks between meals. ☐
5 Take your time when you eat. ☐
6 Don't miss breakfast. ☐
7 Focus on your food. ☐
8 Drink plenty of clear liquids. ☐

3 Read the text on page 25 quickly. Match the advice from exercise 2 to each paragraph.

HEALTHY EATING

Your body needs energy and nutrients from food to grow and work properly. If you don't eat a healthy, balanced diet, you could be putting your health and growth at risk.

A healthy diet also gives you the energy you need and can help you look and feel great. But eating well doesn't have to mean cutting out all your favourite food. A healthy diet means eating a wide range of food so that you get all the nutrients you need and eating the right number of calories for how active you are.

HERE'S A QUICK GUIDE

A ......

Some people skip the first meal of the day, but doing this is not good for you because you can miss out on essential nutrients. It's an important part of a balanced diet and provides some of the vitamins and minerals we need for good health.

B ......

They are good sources of many of the vitamins and minerals your body needs. It's not as hard as it might sound: fresh, frozen, tinned, dried and juiced fruit and vegetables all count towards your total. So fruit juice without extra sugar and smoothies count.

C ......

Foods high in fat include pizzas, chips, burgers, biscuits and crisps. Foods high in added sugars include cakes, sweets and chocolate. Both fat and sugar are high in calories, so if you eat these foods often, you're more likely to become overweight.

D ......

If you're hungry between meals, eat food such as wholemeal bread, beans, wholegrain breakfast cereals, fruit and vegetables. Foods that are high in fibre fill us up and help us to feel full for longer, and most of us should be eating more of them.

E ......

Aim for six to eight glasses per day: water, fruit juices without extra sugar (mixed with water) and milk are all healthy choices.

F ......

The labels you see on food can seem a bit boring, but they are the best way of checking what you're eating as they can tell you what's hidden inside the food. Once you know how to use them, you'll soon be able to make healthier choices when you buy food.

G ......

It takes time for our brains to understand that we're full, so try to eat more slowly. If you're eating with friends or family, try eating at the same speed as the slowest eater. You'll enjoy your food more, too.

H ......

Eating while doing something else, such as watching TV or playing on your tablet, means we eat more without noticing or even enjoying it. Swap the TV for the table.

---

4 Read the text again. These sentences are all false. Use the information in the text to correct them.

1 It's better to miss breakfast than lunch.

....

2 Very sweet food is likely to be high in fat.

....

3 We should drink lots of tea and coffee during the day.

....

4 We should eat our meals as fast as possible.

....

5 Find the words or phrases in the text which mean the following.

1 a healthy mixture of different types of food (introduction) ....

2 not do something that you usually do or that you should do (paragraph A) ....

3 where something comes from (paragraph B) ....

4 substance taken from animals or plants and used in cooking (paragraph C) ....

EP **Word profile** *live*

Complete the sentences with *for, on* or *up to*.
1 Mrs Duke's dog lives .... steak. He won't eat anything else!
2 I'm afraid the new restaurant didn't live .... our expectations.
3 I don't really care about football, but my sister is the opposite – she lives .... it.
4 It's really difficult to live .... 100 euros a week.

GRAMMAR Present perfect and past simple

1 Choose the correct answers.

1 I *read* / *'ve read* over 12 books since the start of this year.

2 Let's go to a restaurant tonight – we *didn't eat* / *haven't eaten* out for weeks.

3 What *did you cook* / *have you cooked* for dinner last night?

4 Daniel *went* / *has gone* for a run and he isn't back yet.

5 I'm not hungry because I *just have* / *'ve just had* a big lunch.

6 She still *didn't find* / *hasn't found* the recipe she's looking for.

7 We *often helped* / *have often helped* in the kitchen when we were children.

8 *Did you finish* / *Have you finished* your maths homework yet?

2 Complete the conversations with questions in the present perfect or past simple.

0 A: How long / you / be / a chef?
....How long have you been a chef......... ?

B: It'll be two years next month.

1 A: What time / you / eat / lunch?

....

.... ?

B: One o'clock.

2 A: you / try / the new café / yet?

....

.... ?

B: No, not yet.

3 A: you / enjoy / the meal?

....

.... ?

B: Yes, it was great.

4 A: How many / cups of coffee / you / have / today?

....

.... ?

B: Let me think – four! That's too many!

5 A: Where / you / find / your mobile?

....

.... ?

B: In my bag. It was there all the time.

6 A: How / the weather / be / recently?

....

.... ?

B: Awful, I'm afraid.

7 A: you / see / this TV show / before?

....

.... ?

B: Yes, several times.

8 A: James / call you / yesterday evening?

....

.... ?

B: Yes, but I couldn't speak to him.

3 Complete the email with the verbs in brackets in the correct form.

Dear Barry

Thank you so much for the international recipe book that you [1] .... (give) me for my birthday last week. I [2] .... (already / use) it three times! All the meals I [3] .... (make) so far have been delicious.

Last night I [4] .... (cook) a Japanese dish and tomorrow I'm going to try an Ethiopian recipe. Nobody in my family [5] .... (ever / eat) Ethiopian food before, so they are all looking forward to it. [6] .... (you / try) it before? [7] .... (you / enjoy) it?

See you soon!

Tina

4 Complete the conversation with the verbs in brackets in the correct form.

A: [1] .... (you / see) that new burger place in the shopping mall?

B: Yes, I have. I know it well.

A: How long [2] .... (be) there?

B: I think it [3] .... (be) open for about a month. That's right, it [4] .... (open) just before I [5] .... (go) on holiday last month.

A: [6] .... (you / try) it yet?

B: Well, I [7] .... (eat) there once, and Jane and I [8] .... (already / spend) a few hours in there with drinks – the atmosphere's quite good, but the burger I [9] .... (have) there [10] .... (not be) great.

A: Oh, OK. Maybe I'll try it.

5 ⊙ Correct the mistakes in these sentences or put a tick (✔) by any you think are correct.

1 I realise how tired you must be after the long journey you had. ....

2 How has modern technology changed your daily life? ....

3 I have worked on a farm in Turkey last summer. ....

4 In my opinion this is one of the best movies I've ever seen and it was already nominated for several awards. ....

5 I have been very disappointed when I read your advertisement. ....

6 He is the greatest person I know because he is always there for his family and still achieved a lot in his career. ....

VOCABULARY Forming adverbs

1 **Write the adverb formed from the adjective.**

1 accidental ....
2 basic ....
3 beautiful ....
4 brave ....
5 complete ....
6 considerable ....
7 enthusiastic ....
8 extreme ....
9 happy ....
10 incredible ....
11 necessary ....
12 physical ....
13 terrible ....
14 typical ....

2 **Match some of the adverbs in exercise 1 to these meanings.**

1 in a pleased way ....
2 in a way that shows all the characteristics expected from a person, thing or group ....
3 by chance or mistake ....
4 very badly ....
5 in a very interested and eager way ....
6 in a way that is very attractive ....
7 in every way or as much as possible ....
8 in a way that relates to the body or someone's appearance ....
9 in a way that shows no fear of danger ....
10 used in negatives to mean *in every case* or *therefore* ....

LISTENING

1 ▶4 **Listen to four short recordings. Where do they take place? Match them to the pictures. (Be careful!)**

1 .... 2 .... 3 .... 4 ....

2 ▶4 **Listen to the recordings again and choose the correct answers.**

1 The girl buys bananas and
   a apples. b oranges.
2 The girl says that her first day at her new job was
   a frightening. b tiring.
3 The reviewer thought the book
   a would be better with pictures.
   b was bit disappointing.
4 The boy knew about the café because
   a he had read about it.
   b a friend had told him.

3 **Look at the conversation below. Try to fill in the gaps.**

Tonia: It's my birthday next month, and I want to invite a few friends out for a meal. My parents are paying!
¹ ....
any good restaurants?

Marco: I know a few. What kind of food do you want?

Tonia: I haven't really thought about it. Something that everyone will like.

Marco: ² .... asking your friends what they like first?

Tonia: That sounds
³ ....

Marco: Or you could just go to a pizza restaurant. Everybody likes pizza.

Tonia: That's an even better idea! We'll go to Pizza Box.

Marco: Hmm. ⁴ ....
of Pizza Box. It's expensive and the service isn't very good. And
⁵ ....
going to Balotelli's – that's even worse.

Tonia: Well, ⁶ ....
good pizza places?

Marco: Hmm, ⁷ ....
Mario's. The pizzas are great, the service is good and it's not too expensive.

Tonia: That ⁸ ....
– thanks!

Marco: Oh, by the way, am I invited?

Tonia: Of course!

4 ▶5 **Now listen to the conversation and check your answers.**

VOCABULARY   Fiction: adjectives and nouns

1 Write the words in the box below into the correct column.

> character   complex   contemporary   factor
> flavour   issue   key   major   minor
> moving   outstanding   plot   role   tale
> treatment   unpredictable

Nouns	Adjectives

2 Complete the sentences with nouns from exercise 1.

1 Money was a key .... in his decision to write his life story.
2 I knew he was a major .... in the play because his name was the same size as the title on the poster.
3 The book has a very contemporary .... , with lots of textspeak and internet language.
4 I only have a minor .... in this play – I'm a pizza delivery boy!
5 The story has such an unpredictable .... that you get a surprise at the end of nearly every chapter.
6 The teacher read us a very moving .... about a child who was brought up by wolves.
7 The outstanding .... of very complex .... is what makes this book so special.

3 Choose an adjective + noun phrase from exercise 1 to complete each of the short texts below.

0 Have you read the latest thriller by R L Stine? It's amazing – you don't know what's going to happen from one page to the next. It's got such an ...*unpredictable plot*... .
1 It's a very sensitive topic but I think the writer handles it brilliantly. In fact, I think she should win a prize for this ....
2 It's unusual for an author so young to attempt to write about such difficult and .... and do it so successfully.
3 The fact that the writer brings in political issues that are happening at the moment gives the book a really ....
4 Everyone says that the book is really popular because it's a fast-moving thriller, but I don't agree. I think it's the really realistic dialogue that is the ....
5 Every now and again I just have to read a book that makes me cry. Sometimes the most important thing for me is that the book has to have a ....

READING

1 How many ways can you think of to read fiction? Look at the photos on page 29 and make a list.

....
....
....

2 Read the article quickly. Is it positive or negative about technology? Does it mention your ways of reading from exercise 1?

....

3 Five sentences have been removed from the article. Choose from the sentences A–F the one which fits each gap (1–5). There is one extra sentence which you do not need to use.

A Cartoon characters like Tintin and Asterix are as popular today as they were when they were first written in the mid-20th century.
B Although teenagers may not be reading books, that does not mean they are not reading.
C You might think that the smaller reading surface of a smartphone or tablet would make it difficult to read long books, but this is not the case.
D As a result the ability to concentrate is being affected and young people have a shorter attention span than their parents and grandparents.
E This variety of digital devices tends to encourage reading rather than discourage it, as the activity can take place anywhere, anytime.
F They are 'digital natives' – that is, they were born at a time when the internet was already part of everyday life and take it for granted.

Do you like reading?

Do you read for pleasure, or only if you have to, for school? Not so long ago, children and teenagers used to read a lot of comics, novels and books of short stories. Sometimes, if the story was really exciting, they were so keen to find out what happened to their favourite characters that they would read under the bedclothes at night with a torch.

However, that was at a time before television was available 24 hours a day. Today's teens also have access to the internet and instead of reading books, as earlier generations did, spend time on social media, messaging and chatting to their friends. [1] At least that's what many people believe, but recent research suggests something different.

In contrast to what a lot of older people think, teens don't in fact just use new technologies to talk to their friends. [2] A World Book Day survey of teenage reading habits revealed over 40% read books on a computer, almost 20% on a mobile device and around 14% on a tablet, with around 10% reading on an e-reader.

Why should this be? Well, the British telecommunications supervisor Ofcom points out that children as young as six understand digital technology better than adults. [3] Teens today have never known a time without the internet, so it is as natural to them to use internet-enabled devices as it was to their parents to use books.

So, what are teenagers reading? [4] Today's teens still like to read the classics as well as modern fiction and have no difficulty in reading them on a digital device. Adventure, crime and spy stories are all popular, with some authors like John Grisham and Ian Rankin as popular among teens as adults. Among the classics Charles Dickens remains a favourite, along with Jules Verne and Alexandre Dumas.

The classics do not only include novels. [5] It isn't only older comic-style books that are proving popular with teens these days either, but the modern-day comic, the graphic novel, is gaining in popularity everywhere. So it seems there is no danger of young people losing the habit of reading any time soon!

4 Underline the parts of the text which gave you the answers. This has been done for the first gap.

5 Write questions about the article, for these answers.

0 ..Why did children use to read under.......... ...the bedclothes with a torch?.........................
Because they were keen to continue their book.

1 ....
That smartphones, tablets and other digital devices affect concentration.

2 ....
Because they've never known a time without the internet.

3 ....
John Grisham and Ian Rankin for example.

4 ....
The graphic novel.

EP Word profile *story*

Complete the sentences with the words in the box.

| another | contemporary | fairy | long |
| main | news | short | side |

1 I've always enjoyed reading .... stories – they're so magical.

2 To cut a .... story short, I eventually got home about 3.00 in the morning!

3 The big earthquake in China was the first .... story on TV last night.

4 Many successful novelists start their careers by writing .... stories in fiction magazines.

5 I told the police my .... of the story, and they let me go.

6 Her first novel was terrible, but her next one was .... story – it was brilliant!

7 It's a very .... story. It takes place at the Olympics in Tokyo.

8 The .... story from Wimbledon today is the exit of the world number 1.

GRAMMAR Modals: Ability, possibility and *managed to*

1 Choose the correct answers. Sometimes two answers are correct.

1 I .... swim until I was fifteen years old.
   a couldn't   **b** managed to
   c wasn't able to

2 How .... fix Mark's computer?
   a could you   **b** did you manage to
   c managed you to

3 Stella could read before she .... walk.
   a was able to   **b** could
   c might be able to

4 Tom has hurt his leg, so we .... play tennis next weekend.
   a won't be able to   **b** couldn't
   c didn't manage to

5 In the end, I .... persuade my dad to buy me a scooter.
   a was able to   **b** managed to
   c will be able to

6 Tickets are going to be very difficult to get, but with luck we .... buy some on the internet.
   a could   **b** might be able to
   c will be able to

7 .... finish your project in time last week?
   a Did you manage to   **b** Could you
   c Will you be able to

8 It was hard work, but eventually I .... climb over the garden wall.
   a managed to   **b** could
   c was able to

2 Complete the sentences with *(not) be able to* and a verb from the box. Use *might* if possible.

> beat   come   go   help
> mend   play   see   visit

1 I'm not sure yet, but I .... (not) to your party tomorrow.

2 When we climbed to the top of this mountain, we .... the whole city.

3 I think I .... this bicycle – it could be easy, or it could be impossible.

4 When I get a car, we .... anywhere we like at the weekend!

5 I asked Susan for advice, but she .... (not) me.

6 Even if you train every day for a year, you .... (not) me in a 100 metre race!

7 She hopes she .... her grandmother soon.

8 We .... (not) football tomorrow – it depends on the weather.

3 ⊙ Correct the mistakes in these sentences or put a tick (✔) by any you think are correct.

1 He thought he can swim. ....

2 He is so sly that he managed to avoid detection for a long period by pretending to be a good man. ....

3 It was the first time a song could make me cry. ....

4 As I ordered him not to move, I could call the police. ....

5 Even though he was born into a poor family he managed it to go to school. ....

6 We decided to find a job in order to can get the money for Carla's present. ....

VOCABULARY Adjective + preposition

1 Match the prepositions in the box to the adjectives.

> about   at   by   for   in   on   to   with

1 addicted ....
2 annoyed ....
3 disappointed ....
4 furious ....
5 keen ....
6 nervous ....
7 surprised ....
8 suitable ....

2 Complete the sentences with an adjective + preposition from exercise 1.

1 I always get .... exams, and never sleep well the night before.

2 Our teacher gets very .... students talking in class, and sometimes shouts at them.

3 I thought her first novel was great, but I was .... her second one, which wasn't nearly as good.

4 Dan is .... computer games – he just can't stop playing them.

5 My dad was absolutely .... me when I crashed my bicycle into his car.

6 The organisers were .... the number of people who turned up – they weren't expecting so many.

7 This book is quite frightening, so it isn't .... young children.

8 I'm not really .... novels, but I read a lot of comics.

WRITING A story

See Prepare to write box, Student's Book page 45.

1 Read the task. Is this going to be a happy or a sad story?

> **Send us a story!**
> We are looking for stories to publish on our teenage fiction website. Your story must begin with this sentence:
> *My best friend phoned me on my mobile, sounding very excited.*
> Your story must include:
> • a celebrity   • an invitation

Write your **story**.

2 Make some notes for the story.

1 What did your friend say?
....

2 How did you feel?
....

3 What did you do next?
....

4 What happened?
....

3 Read the story. Is the story similar to your notes? Does it answer all parts of the task?
....

My best friend phoned me on my mobile, sounding very excited. 'You won't believe this,' she said, 'but Scott Moss is at the bookshop in town. He's signing copies of his books.'
I didn't believe her for a long time, but she ¹ .... convinced me she was telling the truth. ² .... I became very excited. Scott Moss is my favourite comic book artist. I've been reading his stuff for years. ³ .... was my big chance to meet him!
'I'll be there as soon as I can,' I told my friend. ⁴ .... I grabbed the latest Scott Moss comic book, and jumped onto my bike. It was raining but I didn't care – I was going to meet the most outstanding comic book artist in the country!
⁵ .... I arrived at the bookshop, my friend came up to me. We joined the queue of people waiting to meet Scott. ⁶ .... my turn came, and I told him about my ambition to be a comic book artist. I couldn't believe it when he invited me to visit him at his studio! What a day!

4 Complete the story with the time expressions below.

as soon as	finally	in the end
that's when	now	then

5 Use your notes from exercise 2 to write your own story.

- Use time expressions to structure your story.
- Remember to check your spelling and grammar.
- Write 140–190 words.

8 Getting away from it all

VOCABULARY Holidays

1 Match the verbs to a preposition in the box to create phrasal verbs.

| around | down | out | out | up | up |

1 chill ....   4 stay ....
2 cool ....   5 try ....
3 sign ....   6 wander ....

2 Choose two correct answers to complete the sentences.

1 Last holiday, I hired .... for an afternoon.
   a a jet ski   b a tour
   c a motorbike
2 We always like to try out .... when we go to a different country.
   a the local food   b the sights
   c some new sports
3 Did you go .... when you were in Spain last year?
   a up all night   b trekking
   c sailing
4 It's a good idea to sign up for .... when you go to a new place.
   a an organised tour   b excursions
   c a tan
5 Last year we went cruising on .... for our holiday.
   a a yacht   b a bus
   c a huge ship

3 Complete the email with the words in the box.

| chill | cool | hired | photographed | signed |
| socialised | stayed | tan | wandered | went |

We have just had a lovely holiday in Spain. We stayed on a quiet campsite near the coast where we could ¹ .... out all day if we wanted. I ² .... a jet ski on the first day, while my parents and sister sunbathed on the beach. In the evening, we ³ .... with the other campers, which was great. On the third day we ⁴ .... up all night! The day after that we were very tired, so we just ⁵ .... around the local town a bit. Then, on the following day, we ⁶ .... up for an organised tour and ⁷ .... the sights. On the day before we left we ⁸ .... trekking in the mountains in the morning, and then before it got too hot we came back to the beach and ⁹ .... down in the sea. We all got a great ¹⁰ .... to show off to our friends at home!

4 Complete the questions, then match them to the answers below.

1 What's your favourite way to .... ?   ....
2 Have you ever .... all night?   ....
3 How do you .... when you're hot?   ....
4 What really unusual food have you .... ?   ....
5 Do you ever .... organised tours on holiday?   ....

a Once, when my parents had a party!
b Cheese and cake together – it's really strange!
c I like closing my eyes and listening to music.
d Yes, but I prefer to wander around on my own.
e I sit with my feet in water – it really works well!

READING

1 Look at the photo. What do you think the family is doing?

....

2 Read the article quickly. Where do you think it comes from?

a a book
b a magazine
c a travel brochure

3 Read the article again and choose the correct answers.

1 What is meant by the phrase 'putting down roots' (line 7)?
   a creating a permanent home
   b making money
2 Why did Mr and Mrs Zapp want to go on a long journey?
   a because their family was unkind to them
   b because their lives did not feel complete
3 How did the relatives of the Zapps feel about their journey?
   a pessimistic
   b optimistic
4 Why do they call their children's education 'worldwide schooling'? (line 29)
   a because they learn a lot of geography
   b because they learn while they are travelling
5 What is the main advantage of travelling in a very old car?
   a It attracts a lot of attention on the road.
   b It allows them to meet new people when it breaks down.

Are we there yet?

Imagine travelling around the world with your family, by car, for 11 years straight. For some it would be like a dream come true. For others, it would get boring pretty quickly. But American couple Herman and Candelaria Zapp, along with their four children – all born on the road – are living the dream.

The couple spent their first few years of married life
7 putting down roots in Argentina, where Herman had his own computer and telephone IT company, and they had a nice house with a swimming pool. 'Our family was happy with us. We had it all,' said Herman Zapp.

But something was missing: that around-the-world trip they had talked about, and children. So, the couple set out on a pre-baby road trip from Buenos Aires to Alaska. But now they didn't get much support. 'Our family was saying that we wouldn't make it,' Zapp said. 'The most optimistic were giving us a week's journey. No more.'

Not only did the couple complete their nearly 44,000-mile initial journey, but they decided to keep going. Since then, they've been to more than two dozen countries and travelled at least 145,000 miles.

Each of their four children was born in a different country: Pampa in the United States, Tehue in Argentina, Paloma in Canada and Wallaby, the youngest, in Australia. The Zapps educate their kids themselves but also say the experiences they get are incredibly educational. 'Imagine taking your kids and watching the space shuttle take off, looking at polar bears in Alaska, seeing kangaroos in Australia and learning to speak the language of the country you're in,' Zapp said. 'We call it
29 worldwide schooling.'

For their entire 11-year adventure, the Zapps have been traveling in a 1928 car that can't go faster than 40 miles per hour. Part tent, part kitchen, part schoolhouse and part rolling apartment, the car is definitely also a part of the family. They call it 'Grandpa'. 'I am not a mechanic at all, but every time we get a breakdown we get a new friend,' said Zapp. 'Once we broke down in Puebla, a beautiful city in Mexico. When I looked at the engine someone showed up right away and told me about a car museum nearby. We went there and they took apart a car on show to give us the part.' Not only did the museum not charge for that part, but the town organised a party for the Zapps, complete with a mariachi band and plenty of food.

When and where will the road end? The Zapps say they intend to keep going, but may take a break in two years when their oldest son, Pampa, turns 10.

4 **What to these numbers from the article refer to?**

1 11 ....
....
2 44,000 ....
....
3 40 ....
....
4 145,000 ....
....

EP **Word profile** *last*

Choose the correct word to complete the sentences.

1 I haven't seen Bruce since the week .... last.
  a minute   **b** thing   **c** before   **d** least
2 We managed to get tickets because there was a last-....... cancellation.
  a minute   **b** thing   **c** before   **d** least
3 The last .... you need when you're on a long journey is for the car to break down.
  a minute   **b** thing   **c** before   **d** least
4 And now, ladies and gentlemen, last but not .... , is our final act of the night!
  a minute   **b** thing   **c** before   **d** least

GRAMMAR Future (1): Plans and intentions

1 **Delete the adverb which is in the wrong place.**

0 We *probably* won't ~~*probably*~~ have time to visit all the sites in one week.

1 *Definitely* I will *definitely* email you as soon as I arrive.

2 You *certainly* aren't *certainly* going to need any warm clothes when you visit us in Jamaica!

3 He *probably* will *probably* be back by the end of the month.

4 *Certainly* I will *certainly* enjoy my trip to New York this summer.

5 It's *definitely* not *definitely* going to rain this afternoon.

2 **Choose the correct answer.**

1 **A:** It's cold in here.
   B: OK, I *'ll* / *'m going to* close the window.

2 **A:** Our train *will leave* / *leaves* at 4.45. We need to hurry.
   B: That's OK. I *'ll drive* / *'m driving* you to the station.

3 **A:** I *'ll go* / *'m going to go* swimming after school. Do you want to come?
   B: Sure! I *'m going* / *'ll go* home and get my stuff.

4 **A:** Oh, good. You're packing. *Are you taking* / *Will you take* some warm clothes with you?
   B: No way, Mum. I've seen the weather forecast. It*'s being* / *'s going to be* really hot!

3 **Complete the sentences with the correct future form and your own ideas.**

1 **A:** Can I get you something to drink?
   B: Yes, please. I ....

2 **A:** What do you want to study at university?
   B: I've made up my mind. I ....
   ....

3 **A:** Dinner will be ready at 7.00. Don't be late.
   B: But I can't have dinner with you!
   I ....

4 **A:** Do you want to come camping with us this weekend?
   B: Sorry, I'd love to but I can't. I ....
   ....

5 **A:** I don't feel very well. I feel dizzy.
   B: Sit down. I ....

4 ◉ **Correct the mistakes in these sentences or put a tick (✔) by any you think are correct.**

1 She's going to have a good time at the party, I think.
   ....

2 I am sure that you will enjoy yourselves very much. ....

3 Please let me know what you will do next week.
   ....

4 I will cook something special from my country and I am sure that you would like it! ....

5 We will discuss it when you will come home.
   ....

VOCABULARY Phrasal verbs: travel

1 **Complete the phrasal verbs with the correct preposition. Then complete the definitions with a word or phrase from the box.**

bill	holiday	home	~~key~~	leaving
look at	place	show	stop	

0 check ....*in*.... : arrive and get the ...*key*... at a hotel

1 check .... : pay the .... , return your key, and leave a hotel

2 get .... : travel or move from place to ....

3 get .... : to go on .... , often because you need a rest

4 look .... : visit a place and .... the things in it

5 see .... : to go where someone is .... and say goodbye

6 stay .... : .... somewhere briefly during a longer journey

7 stop .... : spend the night somewhere other than ....

8 take .... : .... someone the best parts of a certain place

2 **Complete the sentences with phrasal verbs from exercise 1.**

1 She's been working very hard and needs to .... for a few days.

2 We .... the island on motorbikes we hired for the week.

3 Sally is .... at her best friend's house this evening.

4 It's too far to drive in one day, so we'll .... in Las Vegas for the night.

5 After I had .... at the hotel, I went up to my room and slept for five hours.

6 I'll come and .... you .... at the airport tomorrow.

7 An hour after I .... , I realised I'd left my mobile charger in the hotel room.

8 I've never been to this city before, so I'd like to find someone to .... me ....

9 Let's .... this place for a while before we decide whether or not to stay here.

LISTENING

1 Look at the web page. Who writes it? What's it about?

....

AROUND THE WORLD *with Sally*

BLOG	ABOUT	GALLERY	CONTACT

2 Imagine you are going to interview Sally, the owner of the web page. What questions would you ask her?

....
....
....
....

3 Now look at the multiple-choice options in exercise 4. Could any of the questions you thought of in exercise 2 fit below?

4 ▶6 Now listen to the interview with Sally and write in the questions. (Write *Sally* rather than *you*.)

1 ...*Why did Sally start writing her blog in the first place*........... ?
   A to help her remember her travels   **B** to share her experiences with others
   C to encourage others to do the same as her

2 .... ?
   A the journey from place to place   **B** experiencing the lifestyles in different countries
   C meeting other travellers

3 .... ?
   A when she first went abroad with her parents   **B** when she first worked in another country
   C when she was in a country for a long enough time

4 .... ?
   A not to stick to a strict schedule   **B** to plan your trip carefully
   C to sort out the practical details before you leave

5 .... ?
   A to continue studying for another year   **B** to work for her father
   C to work for herself

5 ▶6 Listen to the interview again and choose the best answer, A, B or C.

9 Spend or save?

VOCABULARY Money

1 **Choose the correct answer.**

1 You'll never be *financially independent / short of cash* if you don't get a job.
2 We're on a very tight *debit card / budget* this holiday because we spent a lot on the flights.
3 How much money did you *pay off / take out* of the cashpoint today?
4 A family can't *pay off / live on* so little each month.
5 I've finally *paid off / taken out* that large credit card bill from the holiday.
6 Sorry, I can't come out tonight – I'm really *wealthy / short of cash*.
7 I need to check my *balance / budget* at the cashpoint before I buy these clothes.
8 Two burgers for the price of one – I call that a *budget / bargain*.
9 I needed to get some money but the *cashpoint / PIN* was empty.
10 Do your parents give you *an allowance / savings* every week?

2 **Match the descriptions to words or phrases in exercise 1.**

1 This is the amount of money you have in your account. ....
2 Perhaps you get this from your parents every week? ....
3 Your parents probably get this at the end of every month, then they have to pay it. ....
4 This is a number that is for you only; you use it to get money out. ....
5 You have these when you keep money for a particular purpose e.g. to buy something special. ....
6 You can often get this is in a shop that is closing down, when it wants to sell everything. ....
7 Most people get one of these when they open a bank account. They can get money out with it. ....
8 This word describes someone who has plenty of money, more than they need. ....
9 This is a very useful machine that you find outside banks. ....
10 This is what you'll be if you spend more money than you earn every month! ....

READING

1 **You will read about five young people who have become financially independent by making and selling things. Match these general photos with the products they made.**

1 cooking videos   ....
2 a mobile phone game app   ....
3 bow ties   ....
4 a board game   ....
5 hair products   ....

2 **Look at the photos. Which product do you think makes the most money?**

....

Young business people

Check out our list of young businesspeople who became successful before they could drive a car!

A — Leanna Archer – Leanna's Hair

Leanna Archer was just nine years old when she began bottling and selling her own hair gel to friends and family. Based on her great-grandmother's secret recipe, Archer's line of all-natural hair products has expanded to include a variety of hair cleansers, conditioners and treatments. Now the 17 year old is the boss of her own company and has been recognised by prominent business publications like *Forbes* and *Success Magazine*. She even started the Leanna Archer Education Foundation to help build schools and safe learning environments for children in Haiti.

B — Robert Nay – Nay Games

In December 2010, a new mobile game app called *Bubble Ball* was launched on the Apple app store. In its first two weeks it received more than one million downloads, beating *Angry Birds* to become the number one free app on the App Store. This game was coded entirely by Robert Nay, a 14 year old with no previous experience in writing mobile apps. He learnt everything he needed to know through research online, and produced 4,000 lines of code for his physics-based puzzle game in just a month and a half. The teen entrepreneur now runs his own company, Nay Games, which has released many new levels for *Bubble Ball* and has created other mobile apps.

C — Lizzie Marie Likness – Lizzie Marie Cuisine

Like many little girls, Lizzie Marie Likness wanted to ride horses. When she was six years old, she started selling homemade cakes and biscuits at her local market in order to pay for riding lessons. Eventually she realised that cooking was her true passion, and with Dad lending a helping hand, she built a healthy-cooking website with instructional videos to help other kids eat better. Now 15, Lizzie is in college part-time. She has appeared on national TV, and continues to make videos in which she demonstrates her own healthy recipes to kids and parents.

D — Moziah Bridges – Mo's Bows

Most young boys can't stand the idea of getting dressed up, but Moziah Bridges is a rare exception. After being disappointed in the bow ties available to him on the market, Bridges learned how to sew his own with the help of his grandmother. The 11 year old began selling his creations on the internet, and his products were soon picked up by shops all over the country. So far, Bridges has earnt over $30,000 from his bow ties and says that he eventually plans to start a children's clothing company.

E — Anshul Samar – Elementeo

When he was nine, Anshul Samar loved playing card games. Two years later, he began developing his own game, which he called *Elementeo*. Samar aimed to make chemistry fun with his board-based game, in which elements from the periodic table have their own personalities. Since the first version of Elementeo, which made one million dollars in its first year, Samar, now a 19-year-old university student, has continued to update the game. He has also created a fund to help other young entrepreneurs.

---

3 Read the text and answer the questions with A, B, C, D or E.

Which young business person

1 taught themselves the necessary skills alone? ....
2 started the business to fund another activity? ....
3 is involved in building schools? ....
4 was assisted by a parent? ....
5 made a lot of money very quickly? ....
6 started because they didn't find what they wanted? ....
7 gave their product away for nothing at the beginning? ....
8 has had their business skills publicly praised? ....

EP Word profile *account*

Complete the sentences with the words in the box.

into	of	open	on	an

1 I'm going to .... a bank account to save up for university.
2 Have you taken .... account the money you spend on food each month?
3 She forgot to take account .... the extra time she would need to spend on homework.
4 The explorer gave .... account of his journey into the Amazon jungle.
5 Sam's staying in bed today .... account of his cold.

GRAMMAR Future (2): Predictions

1 Match the examples 1–5 with the meanings a–e.

1 This city will become more crowded in the future. ....

2 You might find that you enjoy this game more as time goes on. ....

3 I'm going to pass all my exams this year – I've studied really hard. ....

4 You'll be living in a different country this time next month. ....

5 Dan may well be late home this evening – he's got football training. ....

a a strong possibility in the future
b a possibility in the future
c a general prediction about the future
d a prediction about something in progress in the future
e a prediction based on something we already know

2 Choose the correct future form.

1 I *'ll watch / 'll be watching* that new show on TV at 8.15 tonight.

2 Don't tell Steven your bad news. He won't *like / be liking* it.

3 This time next week, you*'ll lie / 'll be lying* on a beach in the sunshine.

4 I don't think this new product *will sell / will be selling* very well.

5 Don't buy her that book. She *might / could* not like romances.

6 Have a taste of this sauce – you *'re going to / may well* like it even though it's very spicy.

3 Complete the second sentence so that it has a similar meaning to the first. Use the word given.

1 Perhaps we'll meet up later.
MIGHT
We .... later.

2 I think it's very possible that Danny will forget to invite somebody.
WELL
Danny .... to invite somebody.

3 You might become quite rich because of your business idea.
MAKE
Your business idea
.... quite rich.

4 Attending university is not something she plans to do.
GOING
She .... to university.

5 At this time, she'll still be awake.
SLEEPING
She .... at this time.

4 👁 Correct the mistakes in these sentences or put a tick (✔) by any you think are correct.

1 After that, you will be going to have lunch.
....

2 We should use the bicycles for travelling around, because we will be having more fun.
....

3 I will be waiting for you next week. ....

4 September is not suitable for me because I will take examinations. ....

5 I'd like to go on holiday in the summer because I will study in September. ....

VOCABULARY a / the number of

1 Complete the sentences with *a* or *the*.

1 There have been .... number of complaints.

2 She was delighted with .... number of cakes she sold at the fair.

3 .... number of people are joining the club.

4 I couldn't believe .... number of students who failed the test.

2 Match the adjectives to their meanings.

1 considerable .... 5 minimum ....
2 growing .... 6 record ....
3 limited .... 7 reduced ....
4 maximum .... 8 unlimited ....

a describing the largest amount allowed or possible
b made less in number
c kept within a particular size, range, time, etc.
d getting bigger in size or quantity
e large or important enough to be noticed
f describing the biggest, best, highest, etc.
g describing the smallest amount allowed or possible
h without any maximum number

3 Complete the sentences. Use an adjective from exercise 2 and *number*.

1 The number of students is getting bigger.
There is a ....
of students.

2 The number of tickets available is not as big as it was.
A .... of tickets are now available.

3 There is no limit to the phone calls you can make.
You can make an ....
of phone calls.

4 A lot of people bought my app.
My app was bought by a
.... of people.

5 Nobody is allowed to buy more than two tickets.
Two is the .... of tickets anyone is allowed to buy.

WRITING   A profile

1 Look at the notes, then read the profile of Emily on the right. Is all of the information included in the profile?

....

> Name: Emily Standing
> Age: 14
> Business: 'Little Jobs'
> Inspiration: needed money for new mp3 player
> First steps: washed cars, painted fences
> Present: employs 2 friends / makes £2000 per month
> Good points: learn lots
> Bad points: hours / tiredness
> Worst ever job: delivering leaflets
> Future: expand into building / be rich!

2 Underline the information as it appears in the text. Is there any extra information?

....

3 Read the profile of Carlos on the right and complete the notes for him.

> Name: Carlos Moreno
> Age: 15
> Business: ....
> Inspiration: ....
> First steps: ....
> Present: ....
> Good points: ....
> Bad points: ....
> Worst ever job: ....
> Future: ....

4 Complete the profile below with information about you. Invent a business idea of your own.

> Name: ....
> Age: ....
> Business: ....
> Inspiration: ....
> First steps: ....
> Present: ....
> Good points: ....
> Bad points: ....
> Worst ever job: ....
> Future: ....

5 Now write your profile. Think about where to begin and end your paragraphs.

Emily Standing is

14 years old and she runs her own 'little jobs' business in her home town in England. 'When I was ten, I needed money for a new mp3 player. My parents aren't wealthy, so I knew I'd have to wait for my birthday, or make the money myself.'

She started by doing small jobs like washing her neighbours' cars and painting fences. Eventually, she got so busy that she was working all weekend, every weekend.

Now she employs two friends to help her and her company makes over £2,000 a month. Not bad for a teenager! The best thing about it is how much she has learnt by doing all those jobs. The worst thing is the amount of time it takes. 'I'm always tired,' Emily says.

In the future she hopes to expand into the building trade. 'I want to be rich before I'm 30!' she says.

Carlos Moreno is

15 years old and he runs his own business called 'Ice Cream Bicycle' in his village in Ireland. 'It started last year during a really hot summer. There was nowhere in the village to buy ice cream – and there were a lot of people who wanted it!'

Carlos borrowed money from his parents to buy an ice-cream maker. Then he downloaded a few ice-cream recipes from the internet and chose the tastiest one. He fitted a cool box to his bicycle and rode around the village, selling his product.

'People love it!' he said. 'I only work in the summer holidays, but I make quite a lot of money. I love selling ice cream! The only bad thing is my legs get tired – and I don't really like ice cream any more! The worst time was when I made about six different flavours, but forgot which one was which!'

In the future he hopes to pass his driving test and buy an ice-cream van of his own. He'll be able to travel further and sell to many more people then.

10 Give me a hand

VOCABULARY   Household tasks

1 **Write the verbs in the box next to the correct nouns.**

clear up	fix/mend	fold	load
put away	sort	sweep	water	wipe

1 .... clothes / sheets / paper
2 .... the floor / the garden path / the streets
3 .... the rubbish / the recycling / your books
4 .... a room / a mess / a problem
5 .... the table / the chairs / the kitchen surfaces
6 .... your clothes / the dinner things / the children's toys
7 .... plants / the garden / the flowers
8 .... the dishwasher / the washing machine / the car
9 .... or .... the TV / your bike / a computer

2 **Choose the correct answers.**

1 I haven't *watered / sorted* the plants for weeks.
2 Will you *sweep / fold* your clothes and *put them away / clear them up* before you go to bed, please?
3 Before we can watch TV, we have to *wipe / sweep* the table and *put away / load* the dishwasher.
4 I hope you *clear up / sort* this mess you're making after you've finished *loading / mending* your skateboard.
5 The floor is dirty – you'd better *water / sweep* it.
6 I've done the washing – can you *sort / load* it into separate piles of your clothes and your sister's clothes?
7 Don't *load / wipe* the dishwasher this morning because the repair man is coming to *load / fix* it.
8 All these plates and dishes are clean. Let's *clear them up / put them away*.
9 Someone has put all of the rubbish in the same bin. Now I have to go through the bin and *clear it up / sort it* into recycling and ordinary rubbish.
10 Meral, can you *sweep / wipe* the path outside the front door before your grandparents come? The trees have dropped leaves all over it.

3 **Choose the two correct verbs in each list.**

1 You can do this to your clothes.
   put away   water   fold
2 You can do this to a room.
   sweep   clear up   load
3 You can do this with a table.
   mend   wipe   sweep
4 You can do this to a dishwasher.
   water   fix   load
5 You can do this with your shirt.
   put away   fold   sort
6 You can do this with toys.
   load   sort   put away
7 You can do this with the floor.
   sweep   wipe   load
8 You can do this with your bike.
   fix   sweep   mend

READING

1 **What kind of jobs can robots do around the house? Make a list.**

....
....

2 **Quickly read the text on page 41. Where do you think it was published?**

a in a technical manual
b on a technology website
c in a science school book

3 **Read the text more carefully and match the paragraph titles to the correct paragraph.**

1 Kitchen robots ....
2 'Telepresence' (remote) robots ....
3 Grass cutting robots ....
4 Social robots ....
5 Robot alarm clock ....
6 Floor cleaning robots ....
7 Toy robots ....
8 Security robots ....

4 **Which robot would you recommend for these people?**

1 'I spend a lot of time away from home, and the house is often empty.' ....
2 'It's my nephew's birthday next month. He's 12 years old.' ....
3 'I'm often late for school in the morning.' ....
4 'My grandma lives a long way from us and often gets lonely. She could also use some help around the house.' ....
5 'I hate making my own food.' ....

Domestic robots

A domestic robot, or service robot, is a robot that is used for jobs around the house. There are only a limited number of models around at the moment, though some people have suggested that they could become more common in the future. Here are some interesting kinds we've found on our search around the web.

A These are the most common and most popular type of domestic robots currently. They move quickly around hard surface flooring and carpets removing dirt and pet hair – avoiding obstacles like furniture and toys, and automatically finding their way around.

B These sophisticated machines allow you to sit back in your garden and watch them do all the work! You just set up a wire line around the area you want to cut, and switch it on.

C These have night-vision cameras that can detect movement. You can programme them to move around inside or outside your house – and if anything suspicious happens, they will automatically video it and send you a text or email to tell you.

D Our favourite example of this type of robot is called UNO. It dances, plays football with you, shoots table tennis balls, sings songs – and it can recognise your voice, so that it obeys only your orders. It looks really cute too! You can also get electronic pets for the younger members of the family.

E These are similar to toy robots, but with a more serious purpose. A lot of them are designed to help older people by providing company and sometimes helping with the household tasks. In the future, we expect to see robots that are able to understand language, have conversations with you, and understand human emotions, so that they know what to do.

F A step up from social robots, these can allow you to visit a distant location and explore it as if you were there. They let healthcare workers check on patients, for example. Also, children who cannot leave their homes because they are ill or disabled can attend school using one of these!

G You need a highly specialised robot if you want it to do the cooking for you. The one we saw was developed by a German university. It can cook pancakes and sausages, and even make sandwiches. We're not so sure about this one – you might want to supervise if it's using the cooker! You don't want the house to burn down!

H Our favourite of the bunch, this one is for people who can't get out of bed in the morning. It can be set to let you sleep a bit longer, but after that – when your extra time is up – it will scream loudly. If that doesn't work, it will jump off the bedside table and roll around the room flashing its lights and making a noise until you finally get up!

EP Word profile *hand*

Match the phrases with *hand* to their meanings.

1 We hardly ever wash the dishes by hand any more. ....
2 Can you give me a hand clearing up this mess? ....
3 I got into trouble for forgetting to hand in my homework. ....
4 My sister and I walked hand in hand home from the cinema. ....
5 Our teacher handed out our project assignments this morning. ....
6 We had to hand over our mobile phones at the door. ....
7 On the one hand, domestic robots are expensive. On the other hand, they are very sophisticated machines. ....

a give a piece of written work to a teacher
b done or made by a person instead of a machine
c some help, especially to do something practical
d give someone or something to someone else
e holding each other's hands
f give something to each person in a group or place
g used when you are comparing two different ideas or opinions

GRAMMAR The passive

1 **Complete the sentences with the correct passive form of the verb in brackets.**

1 Millions of domestic robots
.... (made) since the
beginning of the century.
2 New technologies which can help with household
tasks .... (develop)
at the moment.
3 Robots .... (use) in
almost every household in the future.
4 The first successful robots
.... (create) in Japan
in the 1980s.
5 Some people think that great chefs
....
(cannot / replace) by robots, because good cooking
is too complicated.
6 Most of the housework in this house
.... (do) by me!
7 This laboratory is totally modern and all of the
experiments now ....
(conduct) by robots.
8 Robots that clean swimming pools
.... (introduce) into
all of the pools in our town. They really keep the
pools clean!

2 **Rewrite the sentences in the passive.**

1 Somebody told me these computers were cheap!
....
....
2 Parents shouldn't give household tasks to children
under ten years old.
....
....
3 They won't allow you to go out if you don't eat your
dinner.
....
....
4 Someone needs to sweep this floor.
....
....
5 Nobody has cleared up this room for days.
....
....
6 They are not telling us the truth.
....
....
7 People are always telling me what to do.
....
....
8 You must deliver this note to
the head teacher this afternoon.
....
....

3 **Seven of the nine underlined clauses in this text would be better in the passive. Choose which seven and rewrite them in the passive, using *by* if you think it is necessary. The first one has been done for you.**

Somebody has broken into our school! It happened last night. It was a very dark night, but a person who lives nearby saw two men climbing over the gate at about 11 pm. Somebody else called the police. They arrived at 11.15, but they didn't find anybody in the school. It seems that the burglars were very quick. They stole some computers. The police have already arrested two men. The police are questioning them at the moment. I hope it is them!

0 .... *Our school has been broken into!* ....
1 ....
....
2 ....
....
3 ....
....
4 ....
....
5 ....
....
6 ....
....

4 ⊙ **Choose the correct sentence in each pair.**

1 a In the advertisement it is said that the cost of
two nights is cheaper.
 b In the advertisement it says that the cost of two
nights is cheaper.
2 a At last, the concert was started.
 b At last, the concert started.
3 a I would like to know if the offer includes
weekends or if the cost could be raised at that
time.
 b I would like to know if the offer includes
weekends or if the cost could be raise at that
time.
4 a We went to the football game, which was held
on Saturday.
 b We went to the football game which held on
Saturday.
5 a We would like to ask if some modifications could
be make to the schedule.
 b We would like to ask if some modifications could
be made to the schedule.

VOCABULARY *make, let* and *be allowed to*

1 Complete the sentences with the correct form of *make, let* or *be allowed to*.

1 My parents .... my little brother brush his teeth before he goes to bed.

2 Are you sometimes .... eat your dinner in front of the TV?

3 Why don't you .... him go out? He's done all his homework!

4 I wasn't .... stay out after 10.00 pm until I was 14 years old.

5 I don't want to go on the school camp. Please don't .... me go!

6 Sue's parents .... her buy whatever clothes she likes.

2 Complete the second sentence so that it has a similar meaning to the first sentence, using the word given.

1 Our teacher lets us eat lunch in the classroom.
   ALLOWED
   We .... in the classroom.

2 I was forced by the headmaster to stay behind after school.
   MADE
   The headmaster .... after school.

3 Dan isn't allowed to ride his bike in the street.
   LET
   Dan's parents .... his bike in the street.

4 Why don't you let Carmen go to the party?
   ALLOWED
   Why isn't .... to the party?

5 We can stay here for another half an hour.
   LETTING
   They .... for another half an hour.

6 I don't want to go to piano lessons, but my parents insist that I do.
   MAKING
   My parents .... to piano lessons, even thought I don't want to.

LISTENING

1 Look at the pictures of chores in the table on the right and write them here.

....
....
....
....
....
....

2 ▶7 Listen to four teenagers talking about the household tasks they do at home. Tick (✔) the correct columns.

	Speaker 1	Speaker 2	Speaker 3	Speaker 4

3 ▶7 Listen again and answer the questions.

Speaker 1

1 Who loads the dishwasher?

....

2 Why don't they wash the car?

....

Speaker 2

3 What time of day does he take the dog out?

....

4 Who cleans the bathroom?

....

Speaker 3

5 How often does she have to water the plants?

....

6 Who washes the car?

....

Speaker 4

7 Why doesn't he take the dog out?

....

8 Why doesn't he make much mess?

....

VOCABULARY Technological advances

1 Match the words from the two columns to make compound nouns. One word from a–g is used three times.

1	3d	**a**	car
2	cloud	**b**	classroom
3	driverless	**c**	computer
4	interactive	**d**	electricity
5	touch-screen	**e**	storage
6	virtual	**f**	technology
7	wearable	**g**	whiteboard
8	wireless		
9	tablet		

1 ....
2 ....
3 ....
4 ....
5 ....
6 ....
7 ....
8 ....
9 ....

2 Complete the sentences with compound nouns from exercise 1.

1 .... means that you can access your documents from any computer in the world.
2 If your devices use ...., they don't need to be plugged in!
3 A(n) .... is a very useful tool for teachers.
4 With ...., you can copy models and other objects.
5 .... run on computers, and never crash or go through red lights.
6 Many people use .... these days because you can take them everywhere.
7 A(n) .... in the form of a bracelet can be worn just like a watch.
8 You can attend a .... without leaving your home.
9 ...., which do not use keyboards as much as older computers, are very common.

READING

1 Look at the pictures. Do you know what they what they are or what they represent?

a ....
b ....
c ....
d ....

2 Read the texts on page 45 and match the paragraphs to the pictures.

3 Look at the gaps in text 3. Use the words in brackets to form a word that fits in the gap.

4 Complete the sentences with *DE* (Doug Engelbart), *B&L* (Babbage and Lovelace), *MZ* (Mark Zuckerberg), or *SJ* (Steve Jobs).

1 .... and .... failed to complete higher education.
2 .... did not see their invention complete in their lifetime.
3 .... started their career while still a child.
4 .... got involved in the entertainment industry.
5 .... and .... created something which many people bought.
6 .... and .... had a connection with Apple Computers.

GIANTS OF TECHNOLOGY

1 Doug Engelbart (photo ....)

In an era when computers were as big as the rooms that held them, Doug Engelbart's ideas were very advanced. He invented a lot of things, but without a doubt his most famous invention was the computer mouse.

The son of a radio repairman, Engelbert studied electrical engineering at university, and eventually became a computer researcher.

The first mouse was a wooden shell with two metal wheels, and was demonstrated in San Francisco in 1968. It was called a mouse because the tail came out of the end.

Although over a billion computer mice have been sold, Engelbart never made much money from them. His company sold Steve Job's Apple Inc a licence for the technology for only about $40,000 in 1983.

2 Babbage and Lovelace (photo ....)

Charles Babbage was an English mathematician and Cambridge University graduate who had the idea of using a machine to solve maths problems. Until that time, human beings did maths on paper – and often made mistakes. In the 1830s Babbage developed what he called the Difference Engine, which was the first ever digital computer. It was the size of a small car.

Babbage's computer was programmed by Ada Lovelace, the daughter of a famous poet. She used small cards with holes in them to give instructions to the machine, and is considered by many people to be the world's first computer programmer.

Together they designed a more advanced machine called the Analytical Engine, but it wasn't actually built until 1991, when British scientists created one from Babbage's notes.

3 Mark Zuckerberg (photo ....)

Some kids are **(0)** .....*passionate*..... (passion) about playing computer games. From early on in his **(1)** .... (child), Mark Zuckerberg loved designing them. His parents gave him a lot of **(2)** .... (encourage) for his interest in computers, and by the time he started university, he already had a reputation as a highly-**(3)** .... (skill) programmer.

In 2004, while still a student, he spent most of his time on the **(4)** .... (create) of a free website which he called TheFacebook. It allowed students at his university to keep each other up to date with what they were doing in their **(5)** .... (day) lives. In the summer of that year it grew quickly in **(6)** .... (popular), and soon expanded to include most universities in the United States. In 2006, it was launched **(7)** .... (global) for anyone over the age of 13 to use.

Now called simply Facebook, it has over one billion users, and Mark Zuckerberg is one of the **(8)** .... (wealth) people in the world – even though he left university in his second year.

4 Steve Jobs (photo ....)

Probably the closest thing the computer industry has ever had to a rock star, Steve Jobs achieved success early in life after giving up university before finishing his first year. Steve Jobs and his friend Woz then formed Apple Computer Inc, when Jobs was just 21.

They went on to make the world's best-selling computer, called Apple 2, then another called the Macintosh. Known as the Mac, it was the first personal computer to use a mouse and a graphical interface – like nearly all computers have today.

In the 1990s and 2000s, Jobs was the creative force behind such best-selling gadgets as the iPod, the iPhone and the iPad – as well as helping create award-winning animated films with Pixar Studios.

---

5 Read the texts again. Are these statements about the texts true (T) or false (F)?

1 Doug Engelbart made very large computers. ....
2 Engelbart's father was also involved in technology. ....
3 Babbage made the Difference Engine with the help of his daughter. ....
4 A model of the Analytical Engine was never built. ....
5 Mark Zuckerberg used to charge money to let people use TheFacebook. ....
6 Zuckerberg's social network service has had more than one name. ....
7 Steve Jobs started his business while at university. ....
8 Other companies copied Apple Inc's early products. ....

EP Word profile *end*

Match the phrases with *end* to their meanings.

1 I'm glad these exams are finally at an end. ....
2 She's been waiting for his call for hours on end. ....
3 It's time to put an end to these spelling errors you are making all the time. ....
4 I've got no end of homework to do this weekend. ....
5 The possibilities for using this new technology are endless. ....

a for hours/days, etc. without stopping
b to make something stop happening or existing
c over / finished
d never finishing
e a lot

GRAMMAR Present perfect continuous

1 Write sentences with the present perfect continuous, using these words.

1 You / play / that game / for hours!

....
....

2 Sam and Sara / amuse / themselves / all day.

....
....

3 We need to find out what / cause / the computer to crash.

....
....

4 How long / you / learn / Spanish?

....
....

5 she / cry for long?

....
....

6 No, I / not / use / your computer.

....
....

2 Choose the correct perfect forms.

1 I've *thought* / *been thinking* – we should get a new computer.
2 She's never *used* / *been using* an iPad before.
3 This is the first time they've *visited* / *been visiting* London.
4 The sun has *shone* / *been shining* all day today.
5 Have you *waited* / *been waiting* here for long?
6 Sorry, I haven't *finished* / *been finishing* my homework yet.
7 You look exhausted. What have you *done* / *been doing*?
8 How long have they *known* / *been knowing* each other?

3 Complete the conversation with the verbs in brackets in the present perfect continuous.

A: What's that you're wearing?
B: This? It's a pedometer – it measures the distance I run. It's really useful.
A: Oh. ¹ .... (you / use) it for long?
B: Yes, since I started running. I ² .... (run) every day for two years now.
A: To keep fit?
B: Yes, but I enjoy it. I ³ .... (train) for a half-marathon recently.
A: Wow! How long do you run every day?
B: Well, today I ⁴ .... (jog) for about an hour, but I'm going to stop now.
A: Oh, good. I ⁵ .... (intend) to ask you about my party next weekend. Can we discuss it now?

4 Complete the email with the present perfect simple or continuous of the verb in brackets.

Hi Mary
How are you? I ¹ ....
.... (not hear) from you for ages.
What ² .... (you / do)?
I ³ .... (just have)
some great news! I ⁴ ....
.... (be) accepted at the
university in my home town to study computing.
You know I ⁵ ....
.... (program) computers since I was
twelve years old and I ⁶ ....
.... (want) to build a career
in computers for ages – well now it's time to start
studying seriously!
The trouble is, I'm so excited that I ⁷ ....
.... (not sleep) very
well since I heard. I'm working in a café at the
moment, and I ⁸ ....
.... (arrive) late a couple of times
already. My boss ⁹ ....
.... (already warn) me twice, and
if I'm late again, I'll lose my job. I don't care too
much – I ¹⁰ ....
.... (save) quite a lot of money
already.
I have to go now. Dad ¹¹ ....
.... (ask) me all week to set
up his new printer in his office, so that's what I'm
going to do now. Then I'm going for a bike ride. It
looks like it ¹² ....
.... (rain), because the roads are wet
– but the sun's shining now.
Write soon!
Jackie

5 ⊘ Correct the mistakes in these sentences or put a tick (✔) by any you think are correct.

1 I study English for two years. ....
2 I have been playing football since I was a child, and I like it very much.

....

3 I like children and I have been working in a similar job before. ....
4 I haven't written for so long, but I have been studying for my exams. ....
5 I was thinking about the ideas you suggested, but I haven't decided yet. ....

VOCABULARY Adjective suffixes

1 Look at the nouns and verbs in the box, then write examples of two adjectives with each suffix below.

> accept attract care colour create
> danger dirt end enjoy environment
> fame fashion harm interact mystery
> nature nerve origin rely sand spice
> suit tradition use

1 -able ....
2 -al ....
3 -ful ....
4 -ive ....
5 -less ....
6 -ous ....
7 -y ....

2 Match some of the adjectives in exercise 1 to these meanings.

1 worried or anxious ....
2 not giving enough attention to what you're doing
   ....
3 able to be trusted or believed ....
4 causing hurt or damage ....
5 special or interesting because of not being the same as others ....
6 acceptable or right for someone or something
   ....
7 following customs or ways that have continued in a group of people for a long time ....
8 strange or unknown, and not explained or understood ....

3 Complete the sentences with an adjective from exercise 1.

1 Thank you, we have had a very .... evening.
2 The latest computer game is really .... – you can play with anyone on the internet.
3 Dan is always drawing and writing stories, because he's very ....
4 I prefer .... beaches to rocky beaches.
5 That film seemed .... – it was so long!
6 Do you like .... food?

WRITING A review

See Prepare to write box, Student's Book page 35

1 Look at the definition. What examples of gadgets can you think of?

....

> **gadget (n):** a small piece of equipment that does a particular job, especially a new type

2 Read the task and the review, without putting the paragraphs in the correct order. Does it include all the information required by the task?

> **Gadget reviews wanted**
> Have you bought a new gadget recently? Why not review it for our website? Tell us why you bought it, what you like or don't like about it, and whether you would recommend it.
> We'll publish the best reviews online!

> **A**
> I love it. It has a nice big touch screen which is easy to type on, and it shows the whole conversation when you are texting someone. The camera is quite good too. You can take colour photos, edit them, and then either text them to friends or upload them to Facebook. It's great fun!
>
> **B**
> I recently bought a new phone. I wanted it mainly to text my friends and take photos. I've been asking my parents to buy me a new one for years, but they made me buy my own with my birthday money.
>
> **C**
> On the whole, I'm very happy with my new phone and I would recommend it to anyone, as long as they don't want to use it mainly to make phone calls!
>
> **D**
> The only thing that isn't so great is the actual telephone. The speaker isn't clear and sometimes it's difficult to hear what people are saying.
> But I don't use the phone much, so it doesn't really matter!

3 Write the letters of the paragraphs in the correct order.

1 Introduction ....
2 Positive points ....
3 Negative points ....
4 Conclusion and recommendation ....

4 Write your own gadget review. Use the structure in exercise 3 to help you.

12 My circle of friends

VOCABULARY Personality adjectives

1 Complete the puzzle with personality adjectives. Use the definitions below to help you.

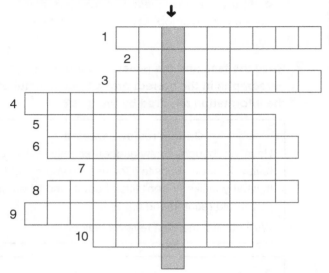

1 easily annoyed by someone's mistakes or because you have to wait
2 not liking to spend money, especially on other people
3 usually relaxed and calm, not worried or upset
4 always believing that good things will happen
5 not able to be trusted or depended on
6 describes a person who becomes angry and annoyed easily
7 able to be trusted or depended on
8 not noticing or not caring about other people's feelings
9 kind and always thinking about how you can help other people
10 being able to stay calm and not get angry, especially when something takes a long time

Word ↓ = ...

2 Choose the correct answers.

1 I know I keep making mistakes. Thanks for being so *impatient / patient* with me.
2 What's wrong with Annie? She seems to be so *easygoing / bad-tempered* these days.
3 He's only 14, but he seems older because he's very *reliable / unreliable* for his age.
4 Sally will share her lunch with you if you forget yours; she's really *generous / mean*.
5 Stop messing around in class – it's so *insensitive / thoughtful* to others.
6 If you can't see the problems here, I think you're too *optimistic / pessimistic*.

3 Complete the sentences with *opposites* of the adjectives below.

> bad-tempered   generous
> insensitive   patient
> pessimistic   reliable

1 You should try to be more .... , because you accidentally hurt people's feelings too often.
2 I wouldn't trust Mark to be part of our team – he's totally ....
3 Don't be so ....! Dinner will be ready in 20 minutes.
4 Danielle is really .... – nothing seems to bother her.
5 I'm quite .... about the weather next weekend. The forecast isn't bad.
6 It was very .... of you not to give your sister a present for her birthday.

READING

1 Read the text quickly. Choose the best title.

a Friendships and older people
b Friends are good for you
c The science of friendship

2 The topic sentences are missing from the article. Write the numbers next to the correct paragraphs.

1 Unfortunately, people don't have as many friends as they used to.
2 It seems that having a supportive social network can result in less stress and therefore better health.
3 So would we be healthier if we didn't have any friends at all?
4 However, friends can also be a *source* of stress.
5 What about people who prefer to be alone?
6 Generally speaking, girls are better at friendships than boys.

Do you have a large circle of friends? Well, lucky you! Many scientists now believe that people with lots of friends live 22% longer than those with hardly any friends. It's even been suggested that having lots of friends may make it less likely that you will catch a cold. I must say I find that hard to believe – surely spending a lot of time with other people means it's more likely you'll get more colds?

A .... Why should this be? We're naturally sociable animals. We need others for our survival – it's genetic. So people with lots of social connections are more relaxed and easygoing, which is related to better health.

B .... Think about it – how do you feel when your best friend says something nasty to you? People we really like can hurt us much more when they make an insensitive comment, or let us down – because they are more important to us.

C .... Definitely not. When it comes to circles of friends, bigger is better. It seems to be a fact that as your social network gets smaller, your health risks get bigger, or so a lot of scientists believe.

D .... Are they at greater risk? Only if they actually *feel* lonely. Interestingly, bad behaviour and ill health among young people is higher among those who state that they are lonely. And for older people who are lonely, the problems are more connected with sleeping badly, which in turn makes them more bad-tempered and anxious.

E .... In stressful situations girls (and women) protect and care for others, and look for others to support them, which produces health benefits by reducing physical and mental stress. Boys (and men) tend not to do that, as male friendships are often more about helping out with practical problems – mending things and so on.

F .... Or perhaps that's as many *real* friends. People, especially young people, have a lot of online friends these days, but the number of people who feel they have someone they can talk to about important subjects has dropped a lot: by nearly one third in the last ten years. There could be many reasons for this sad decline, but to my mind, the most likely is the growth in the internet – both the time we all spend alone with our computers, tablets and phones, and the belief that we are satisfying our social nature with virtual friendships. Not so!

3 **Find words in the text with these meanings.**

1 when someone or something continues to live or exist (paragraph A) ....

2 possibilities of something bad happening (paragraph C) ....

3 relating to the mind (paragraph E) ....

4 be (not) likely to do a particular thing (paragraph E) ....

5 when something becomes less in amount, importance, quality or strength (paragraph F) ....

4 **Answer the questions in your own words.**

1 Why can having friends be good for our health?
....

2 Why do we sometimes get more stressed when with a friend than with someone we don't like?
....

3 What is the difference between male and female friendships?
....

4 Why do people appear to have fewer strong friendships nowadays?
....

EP **Word profile** *touch*

Complete the sentences with the correct form of the words in the box.

| be   button   lose   stay   sense |

1 It's important to try to .... in touch with old friends.

2 I'll .... in touch with you about going on holiday this summer.

3 Unfortunately, I've .... touch with all my old primary school classmates.

4 She was injured and lost the .... of touch in her right hand for a few weeks.

5 The windows of this house can be opened with the touch of a ....

GRAMMAR Zero and first conditionals

1 Complete the sentences with the verb in brackets in the *will* future, the imperative or the present tense.

1 If you eat all that cake, you .... (feel) ill.

2 If you leave ice cream in the sun, it .... (melt).

3 If you want to come to the meeting, ... (call) Miranda.

4 Pasta .... (be) disgusting if it is cooked for too long.

5 If you don't cook the pasta for long enough, it .... (be) hard.

6 We .... (go) to the swimming pool if it's sunny tomorrow.

7 You .... (be) more likely to be ill if you have no friends.

8 If you want to sleep well, ... (not use) a computer just before going to bed.

2 Complete the second sentence so that it has a similar meaning to the first sentence, using the word given. Write between two and five words.

1 Can I borrow your bicycle and give it back to you this afternoon?
LEND
If ...., I'll give it back to you this afternoon.

2 If Sara eats peanuts, she gets really ill.
CAUSE
Peanuts .... really ill.

3 You won't have any friends if you're mean and insensitive.
BE
Nobody .... if you're mean and insensitive.

4 You say you're feeling ill, so you shouldn't go to school.
IF
Do .... you're feeling ill.

5 Let's move to the countryside – that will probably make me happier.
MIGHT
I .... we move to the countryside.

6 Lying in the sun for too long causes sunburn.
GET
We .... in the sun for too long.

3 Complete the sentences using the zero or first conditional. Use your own ideas.

1 If I eat too much fruit, ...

2 I'll be very happy ....

3 If I want to relax, ...

4 Our teacher gets annoyed ....

4 ⊙ Correct the mistakes in these sentences or put a tick (✔) by any you think are correct.

1 If we stay in the Swan Hotel, we eat there. ....

2 Drop me a line if you can! ....

3 I am a student so I am to earn money, it will be better to work. ....

4 So in the future, using the car will be quite expensive if you drive in one of those towns. ....

5 If you want to visit the sights, you will go to the 'White Tower'. ....

VOCABULARY Adjective and noun suffixes

1 Write the noun or adjective.

1 .... / different
2 fitness / ....
3 .... / generous
4 .... / happy
5 importance / ....
6 .... / intelligent
7 .... / organised
8 patience / ....
9 qualification / ....
10 .... / strong

2 Six of these sentences use an incorrect noun or adjective. Correct the incorrect sentences.

1 It takes a lot of strong to be able to lift your own body weight. ....

2 This is one of the most importance exams you will ever do. ....

3 I'm not very patient – I can't stand waiting long for anything. ....

4 She doesn't want to be involved in the organised of the party, but she wants to be invited. ....

5 Are you happy to teach science to schoolchildren? ....

6 If you want to get fitness, try cycling every day. ....

7 There's not much different between cabbage and spinach. ....

8 Dolphins have much more intelligent than sharks. ....

LISTENING

1 What qualities does a good friend have? Make a list of three or four.

....

....

....

....

2 ▶8 Listen to five people talking about their best friends. Did they mention any qualities in your list?

3 ▶8 Listen again and complete the table with the positive and negative adjectives used to describe the friends.

	Positive adjectives	Negative adjectives
Speaker 1		
Speaker 2		
Speaker 3		
Speaker 4		
Speaker 5		

4 ▶8 Listen again and choose from the list A–H what each speaker says about their best friend. There are three letters which you don't need.

My best friend

A once helped me in a difficult situation.

B sometimes has an attitude which annoys me.   Speaker 1 ....

C can find humour in any situation.   Speaker 2 ....

D is often judged unfairly by people.   Speaker 3 ....

E has a talent which made him popular.   Speaker 4 ....

F gets anxious very easily.   Speaker 5 ....

G did not used to be fond of me.

H is frequently mean to other people.

13 Sports stars

VOCABULARY   Nouns in reporting

1 Complete the crossword using the clues on the right.

Across

4 information that people are talking about although they do not know if it is true

5 when you say that something or someone is bad

7 when you say something that suggests what you think or want, but not in a direct way

10 a statement, often written, that an arrangement or meeting is certain

11 when people have a different opinion about something

12 a suggestion for a plan

Down

1 a brief remark

2 when you say what will happen in the future

3 new information

6 help and encouragement

8 when you admit that you have done something wrong or illegal

9 an argument

2 Choose the correct answers.

1 My best friend and I had a *criticism / quarrel* last week, and we haven't spoken since.

2 We have received *confirmation / confession* by email that the match starts at 3.30.

3 I don't know what to buy Maria for her birthday and she hasn't given me any *hint / rumour*.

4 There was no *mention / prediction* of the tournament in any newspaper.

5 We're looking forward to the *proposal / update* on the progress the team has made so far.

6 My *hint / prediction* for tomorrow's match is a 4–0 win for us.

7 I thought that the coach's *disagreement / criticism* of my playing was very unfair.

8 The tennis player felt that she didn't get enough *confirmation / support* from the crowd.

3 Complete the sentences with the words in the box.

> confession   criticism   disagreement   proposal   rumour   support

1 There's a lot of .... about whether or not to sign a new player to the team.

2 I have a .... to make – I haven't trained for over a month.

3 Steven doesn't take .... very well, so it's best not to say anything bad about his performance.

4 We'd like to thank all our fans for the wonderful .... they have given us this season.

5 Have you read the .... for a new sports hall at school?

6 There's a .... going around that you are leaving the club. Is it true?

READING

1 Read the first part of the article about Jann Mardenborough. Ignore the gaps. What is unusual about the way Jann started his racing career?

....
....
....
....
....
....

2 Complete the first part of the article with the words in the box. There are two extra words that you don't need.

> a   after   back
> because   how   in
> ~~might~~   never   were
> which   with

3 Read the whole article and say whether the statements are true (T) or false (F). Underline the part of the text which gives you the answer.

1 The GP3 racing series is where Formula 1 managers look for talented new competitors. ......

2 Young drivers on the development programme are not permitted to drive new F1 cars. ......

3 Jann will be given the opportunity to do test drives on cars from different F1 teams. ......

4 Jann feels the skills he has acquired will help him at the highest level. ......

5 Andy Damerum believes that the old-fashioned way of getting into Formula 1 will soon be completely replaced. ......

6 Andy Damerum believes that PlayStation racing is an unreliable way to discover new drivers. ......

YOUNG RACERS

Playing video games (0) .... *might* .... be fun – but it will (1) .... get you anywhere. Right? Wrong. Just ask Jann Mardenborough.

The 22 year old from Darlington has just earned a chance to drive for F1 world champion Sebastian Vettel's Red Bull team – and it all started (2) .... of his prowess at the Gran Turismo racing games on the PlayStation.

Mardenborough was the 2011 winner of the GT Academy, a reality TV-style competition (3) .... attracted over 90,000 racing driver wannabees. The early stages of the competition (4) .... played purely on the Playstation, but the best drivers were whittled down until a select few competed (5) .... real-world challenges.

Mardenborough came through to win – and his prize was (6) .... chance to drive for Nissan in the Dubai 24-hour endurance race. He came third in the competition, and hasn't looked (7) .... in his career since: a year (8) .... his big break he won a race in the British GT Championship and came sixth in the season standings.

Last year he was the best rookie in the Toyota Racing Series before earning a chance in both British and European Formula 3 last year. His impressive performances have seen him step up once more for the 2014 season: he will now be racing in the GP3 series, one of the main feeder series for Formula 1.

And what is more, he has been signed to Red Bull's famous young driver development programme, which offers up-and-coming stars the chance to test Formula 1 cars. It's the route that Vettel himself took into F1 – and gives Mardenborough genuine hope of landing a spot in motor racing's premier series. He will have the chance to drive in testing for the most successful team in F1's recent history – and if he shines when given the chance, the sky will be the limit.

Despite having graduated from PlayStation racing less than three years ago, Mardenborough sounds utterly confident about his chances. 'I feel ready for GP3,' he said. 'I've prepared well and I have all the right people around me to help my development so I can fully focus on my racing. Formula 3 has taught me so many things, both in the car and out of the car, both mentally and physically. It was a great stage in my development and I'm sure the skills I've learnt there will help me in GP3 and beyond.'

Red Bull's young driver development manager talked up his new signing, and suggested that there is now nothing strange about unearthing new talent via PlayStation racing. 'We're delighted to welcome Jann onto our programme. We have been tracking Nissan's innovative approach to motorsport, and in particular GT Academy, that challenges the status quo of motorsport,' said Andy Damerum. 'The traditional route to F1 of karting and single-seaters is a tried and tested success, but Nissan and PlayStation have gone down a very different road and started to find some very talented drivers who have been doing all their practising on a games console.'

EP Word profile *shape*

Complete the sentences with the words in the box.

body	good	keep	of	out of	up

1 Sal's in very .... shape because she exercises every day.

2 You have lost every game this season! It's time to shape .... !

3 If you stop training, you'll get .... shape very quickly.

4 She tries to .... in shape by going to the gym twice a week.

5 Tom has the .... shape of a world-class swimmer.

6 They gave Max a birthday cake in the shape .... a tennis racket.

GRAMMAR   Reported statements

1 Tick (✔) the correct statement.

1 Dan said that he had been at the gym.
   a 'I'm at the gym.' ....
   b 'I've been at the gym.' ....

2 He claimed that nobody played the game better than he did.
   a 'Nobody plays the game better than I do.' ....
   b 'Nobody played the game better than I did.' ....

3 She explained that she would help them pack later.
   a 'I'd help you pack later.' ....
   b 'I'll help you pack later.' ....

4 He said he was practising for the following week's match.
   a 'I was practising for the following week's match.' ....
   b 'I'm practising for next week's match.' ....

5 'Hockey is a very physical sport.'
   a Alys said that hockey is a very physical sport. ....
   b Alys said that hockey had been a very physical sport. ....

2 Complete the reported statements

1 'You did very well in the competition.'
   My coach said that I .... very well in the competition.

2 'I'll do my best.'
   Jenny said she .... best.

3 'He's currently the fastest cyclist in the world.'
   Maria said that he .... currently the fastest cyclist in the world.

4 'It's not going to be a very exciting race.'
   Ben warned me that it .... going to be a very exciting race.

5 'I don't want you to injure yourself today.'
   He said that he didn't want me to injure myself .... day.

3 Rewrite the direct speech statement in reported speech.

1 'I've decided to start taking driving lessons.'
   Laura said ....
   ....

2 'He never wanted to be team captain.'
   Alicia told me ....
   ....

3 'Training's always better in the morning.'
   Artur said ....
   ....

4 'I'm feeling exhausted after all that running.'
   Hannah complained ....
   ....

5 'They'll play much better with a new manager.'
   Peter argued ....
   ....

4 ⊙ Correct the mistakes in these sentences or put a tick (✔) by any you think are correct.

1 John said he had some good news to tell me.
   ....

2 She told me that we have only one film left to see.
   ....

3 They told us that the shop will open the following week. ....

4 The next day he rang me and said that we can meet. ....

5 He told us that he can't come because something very urgent had happened. ....

VOCABULARY   Reporting verbs

1 Choose the best reporting verb in the box to report each statement. Two verbs aren't needed.

> admit   beg   confirm   declare
> emphasise   propose   remind   reveal

The rumours are true. I have resigned as manager of the team.

Yes, it was me who told the press about the club's financial situation.

1 ....   4 ....

Please, please, give me one more chance.

Nobody knows this yet – our new signing cost us €5 million.

2 ....

5 ....

I think we should enter both teams in the tournament.

Don't forget that you need to go to your training session today.

3 ....

6 ....

2 Report the statements in exercise 1 using the reporting verbs you chose. You need only report the underlined words.

1 ....

2 ....

3 ....

4 ....

5 ....

6 ....

WRITING An article

See Prepare to write box, Student's Book page 57.

1 Read the task, then read the article below it. Is the style of the article formal or informal?

....

An online sports magazine wants readers to send in articles about their favourite sport.

Tell us about your
favourite sport!

★ Do you like to play it, watch it or both?
★ What are its good points?
★ Does it have any bad points?
★ What health benefits does it offer?
★ Are there any outstanding players?

We'll publish the best articles on our website next month. Send us yours!

BASKETBALL CRAZY

A My favourite sport has to be basketball. As far as I'm concerned, it's the most exciting sport in the world. I love both playing it and watching it. In fact, I'm basketball crazy! I just can't get enough of it.

B What's so great about basketball? For a start, it's great fun to play in a team or on your own, with a basketball hoop in the garden. Not only is it fun to play, but it's also really exciting to watch. It's much faster than football, so you get really fit when you play it. What's more, all that jumping makes your legs really strong.

C I think the outstanding player is Kobe Bryant. He's an incredible athlete, and he's really exciting to watch, though he's getting older now. He plays for a team called the Los Angeles Lakers. On top of all that, he's a really nice guy.

D All in all, I'd recommend you give basketball a try. Go and see a game with a friend, or pick up a ball and shoot a few hoops. You might become basketball crazy, too!

2 Does the article answer all the questions in the task?

....

3 Match the paragraphs in the article to the topics.

1 the star performer   ....
2 introduction   ....
3 getting into it   ....
4 the positives   ....

4 Look at the highlighted phrases in the article. Answer the questions.

Which:

1 emphasises what is really true?   ....
2 introduces a personal opinion?   ....
3 is used to say more than one thing is true?   ....
4 gives the first of several reasons?   ....
5 are used to introduce similar ideas?

....

6 is used to sum up?   ....

5 Read the task again and plan your article using the same structure as the example. Make notes on these topics.

Which sport, and why?
What's good and bad about it?
An example of a star player
How do you start playing?

6 Write your article in 140–190 words. Use informal language.

14 Accident and emergency

VOCABULARY   Accidents and emergencies

1 **Match 1–8 to a–h to make complete phrases.**

1	pass	a	on something sharp
2	have	b	something
3	slip	c	by an animal
4	cut yourself	d	out
5	swallow	e	something poisonous
6	bump	f	your head
7	be bitten	g	an allergic reaction
8	trip over	h	on a wet floor

1 ..d.. .... pass out
2 ....
3 ....
4 ....
5 ....
6 ....
7 ....
8 ....

2 **Complete the sentences with the correct form of verbs from exercise 1 (1–8).**

1 Don't leave that banana skin on the floor – somebody might .... on it.
2 I .... my shoulder as I got out of the car.
3 Have you ever .... by a snake?
4 We had to take my kid brother to hospital because he had .... some ink.
5 Be careful that you don't .... yourself with that knife.
6 When she entered the room she nearly .... over my suitcase.
7 It was so hot in the room that I almost ....
8 I can't eat peanuts because I .... an allergic reaction to them.

3 **Read the speech bubbles and write what happened.**

> **Jane:** Atchoo! I knew coming to a flower show wasn't a good idea!

0 ...Jane had an allergic reaction to flowers...

> **Julian:** Ouch! My head! That ceiling is really low.

1 ....

> **Bob:** Hello, kitty. You're a nice little cat, aren't you? Ow! You horrible animal!

2 ....

> **Emily:** Ooooh! Ouch, my leg. Who left that box in the corridor?

3 ....

> **Paul:** Let me see … chop the onions very finely … Ow! My finger!

4 ....

> **Mum:** Lucy, don't run near the swimming pool. It's wet. Oh no!

5 ....

READING

1 **Look at the title and read the article quickly. What does *accident prone* mean?**

a Having fewer accidents than most people.
b Having more accidents than most people.

2 **Six sentences have been removed from the article. Choose from the sentences A–G the one which fits each gap. There is one extra sentence which you do not need to use.**

A They're thinking about the future or about something that's happened in the past.
B Then, the following week, a guitar fell on my head when I was opening a wardrobe.
C However, he always managed to fight back to health.
D If you're chopping onions with a sharp knife, you have to concentrate on it.
E Nevertheless, the results are encouraging for those who have difficulty doing many things at once.
F Take the sad case of Trevor Cookson.
G Recent research indicates that accident-prone people really do exist.

ACCIDENT PRONE

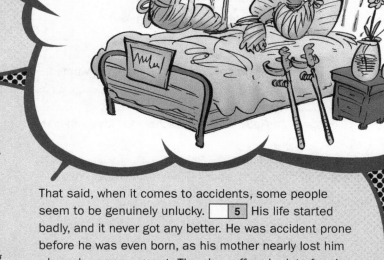

Everyone has accidents from time to time. A bump on the head, a slip on a wet floor – it's almost impossible to go through life without suffering such minor events once in a while. But why do some people seem to suffer accidents more often than others?

Take Kirsty Ball, for example, who considers herself to be particularly accident prone. 'I seem to have more accidents when I'm feeling stressed, or thinking about something,' says the 19-year-old computer programmer. 'Once I slipped on a wet kitchen floor and broke my wrist, and three days later I fell off my bike and hurt my shoulder. ⬜1 I'm sure these things all happened because I wasn't paying attention.'

Danielle Mamby, author of 'Stress and Health', agrees. She believes that people who are stressed aren't 'living in the present'. ⬜2 That's why they aren't paying attention to what's going on around them. 'If you're busy, you go from task to task, and while you're doing one thing, you're thinking about what your next job is going to be,' she says. 'Or you might be thinking about a conversation you had earlier in the day, and wishing you had said something different. Either way, you're not living in the present. You're somewhere else. And that's when accidents happen.'

Science seems to agree with Danielle. ⬜3 Scientists in The Netherlands studied the accidents of nearly 150,000 people from different countries, and found that one out of every 29 people has a 50% or higher chance of having an accident than the rest of the population. So, does that suggest that these people are more stressed than the other 28 in every 29?

No, not necessarily. The scientists concluded that stress wasn't the main factor in causing accidents. 'Stress and anxiety don't help,' says Professor Kurt Knopf, 'but the biggest problem seems to be multitasking – trying to do more than one thing at a time. ⬜4 You can't let things like shouting children or a ringing telephone distract you, or you'll cut yourself.'

That said, when it comes to accidents, some people seem to be genuinely unlucky. ⬜5 His life started badly, and it never got any better. He was accident prone before he was even born, as his mother nearly lost him when she was pregnant. Then he suffered a lot of serious accidents as a child. He broke bones in the playground, and had to have a major operation when he was hurt playing rugby.

As a teenager, he fell from a high wall, then he had a bad bicycle crash just before he started university. That didn't stop him going to university and studying law, though. After he graduated, he worked in a law firm where he had to travel a lot, and as a consequence, broke his back once in a car accident. ⬜6 What's more, he never seemed to be particularly stressed or anxious about anything. In fact, he's now married to a nurse he met when in hospital after breaking his back. 'At least I'm there to look after him when he has another accident', says Simone, his wife, though he's managed the last few years without any accidents at all!

So next time you have an accident, think about Trevor Cookson. He never complained!

EP Word profile *call*

Match the sentences with *call* to the meanings.

1 I wouldn't call that a 'great' film. ....
2 Could you give me a call this evening? ....
3 Somebody is calling my name. ....
4 We're going to have to call off the show. ....
5 He called in on his aunt on the way home. ....
6 What time do you want me to call for you this evening? ....

a visit a place or person for a short time
b decide that a planned event will not happen
c say something in a loud voice, in order to attract someone's attention
d contacting someone by telephone
e to describe something or someone in a particular way
f visit to collect someone

---

3 Choose the correct answer to complete the sentences.

1 Kirsty Ball *understands / doesn't understand* why she has so many accidents.
2 Danielle Mamby believes that people tend to have accidents *when they are very busy / when they are thinking about something else*.
3 Scientists believe that the main cause of accidents is *anxiety / lack of concentration*.
4 Trevor Cookson had a lot of accidents because *he was unlucky / he had a stressful life*.

GRAMMAR Reported questions and requests

1 Write the words in the correct order to make reported questions and requests.

1 was / it / She / him / what time / asked

....
....

2 to know / warm enough / He / if / was / I / wanted

....
....

3 speak / asked / the head teacher / to / My mother / to

....
....

4 they / the kids / where / The police officer / had / been / asked

....
....

5 asked / to help / My sister / me / her

....
....

6 where / The man / me / staying / asked / I / was

....
....

2 Complete the reported questions and requests.

1 'What time did you wake up?'
She asked him what time he ....
....

2 'Please phone for an ambulance.'
The man asked the driver ....
....

3 'Have you started your project yet?'
The teacher asked her ....
....

4 'When are we leaving?'
She asked him when they ....

5 'Are we all going to the park?'
He asked her if they ....
....

6 'Can you help me get out of the car?'
The driver asked the policeman ....
....

7 'Did you hear that strange noise?'
I asked him if he ....
....

8 'What were you doing when it happened?'
She asked him what he ....
....

9 'Can you help me to get up, please?'
The old lady who had fallen asked me ....
....

10 'What on earth has happened in this room?'
Mum came in and asked us ....
....

3 Write the direct speech in the speech bubbles.

1 He asked her if she liked his new bike. She asked him where he had bought it.

2 She asked him to make her a sandwich. He asked her if she had eaten her lunch.

3 He asked her to pick him up. She asked him where he was.

4 She asked him if she could borrow a pencil. He asked her what colour she wanted.

4 ◉ **Correct the mistakes in these sentences or put a tick (✔) by any you think are correct.**

1 She told me that she was with some friends in a restaurant and she told everyone what they wanted for lunch. ....

2 Secondly, you asked me to inform you about our club. ....

3 I was not sure about the decision I should make, so I asked my family what I should do.
....

4 Angela asked Mark what was this light.
....

5 I wanted to know how could I get the magazines or newspapers. ....

VOCABULARY *have, make* and *give* + noun

1 **Match the phrases to the meanings.**

1 make an arrest ....
2 make a comment ....
3 have a fall ....
4 give someone a hug ....
5 have a quarrel/argument ....
6 have respect for someone ....
7 give a sigh ....
8 give someone a welcome ....
9 make a call ....

a hit the ground, often without intending to or by accident
b when police take someone away to ask them about a crime they might have committed
c put your arms around someone and hold them tightly
d meet and speak to a person in a friendly way when they arrive in a place
e express your opinion
f make a sound by breathing out slowly and noisily
g disagree strongly with someone
h be polite to someone, usually because they are older or more important than you
i telephone someone

2 **Complete the sentences with the phrases in exercise 1. Use the correct form of the verbs.**

1 My aunt .... a ....
the other day, and bumped her head.
2 I .... a big .... when
they told me the practice was cancelled again.
3 .... me a ....!
I'm feeling sad.
4 Darren .... a stupid ....
about Sue's dress, and she left the party early.
5 I .... a lot of ....
for people who work in hospitals.
6 The travellers were .... a warm
.... when they arrived in the village.
7 Have you .... a ....
with your sister again? She looks upset.
8 Can I borrow your phone, please? I need to
....
9 Fortunately, the police ....
no .... during yesterday's
football match.

LISTENING

1 **Match the words in the box to the pictures.**

> cut finger   broken tooth   broken arm
> bruised thumb   broken leg

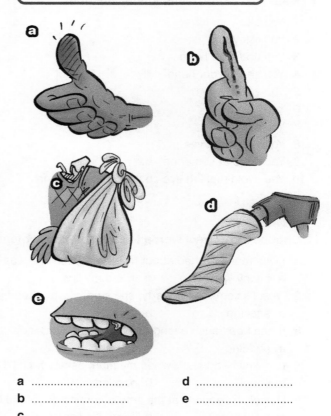

a .... d ....
b .... e ....
c ....

2 ▶9 **Listen to five people talking about an accident they had. Match the speakers to the pictures.**

Speaker 1 .... Speaker 2 .... Speaker 3 ....
Speaker 4 .... Speaker 5 ....

3 ▶9 **Listen again and choose from the list what each speaker says about the cause of the accident. There are three extra letters which you do not need to use.**

A using the wrong tools
B lack of concentration   Speaker 1 ....
C my own foolish behaviour   Speaker 2 ....
D another person's mistake   Speaker 3 ....
E my lack of skill   Speaker 4 ....
F bad luck   Speaker 5 ....
G trying too hard
H being unaware of a dangerous situation

4 ▶9 **Listen again and complete these phrases with the nouns you hear.**

1 I made a ....
2 we didn't have an ....
3 that doesn't stop me having a ....
4 it made a ....
5 I had quite a ....

15 Telling the truth

VOCABULARY Facial expressions

1 Match the expressions to the situations.

1 You bite your lip	....	**a** when you're tired.
2 You lick your lips	....	**b** when you don't stop looking at them.
3 You nod your head	....	**c** when you feel nervous.
4 You shake your head	....	**d** when you don't want to start a conversation
5 You yawn	....	with them.
6 You blush	....	**e** when you are about to eat something delicious.
7 You blink	....	**f** when you agree.
8 You rub your eyes	....	**g** when you're embarrassed.
9 You stare at someone	....	**h** when they are tired or itchy.
10 You avoid making eye contact with someone	....	**i** when you disagree.
		j when you suddenly see a bright light, or you have something in your eye.

2 Choose the correct words to complete the sentences.

1 I was really worried about my sister when she was ill, but I .... and tried not to show my feelings.
   a bit my lip   **b** licked my lips
2 'Yes, I'll come to the party,' she said, ... her head enthusiastically.
   a shaking   **b** nodding
3 It had been such a long day that he couldn't stop ....
   a nodding   **b** yawning
4 I .... my head sadly when my mum asked me if I'd won any prizes that day.
   a shook   **b** nodded
5 Daniel .... eagerly at the smells coming out of the kitchen.
   a bit his lips   **b** licked his lips
6 She .... when she got the answer wrong.
   a blushed   **b** yawned
7 Steve was in class, but I .... because we'd had a huge quarrel the day before.
   a stared at him   **b** avoided making eye contact with him
8 Her eyes were red because she had been .... them.
   a rubbing   **b** blinking
9 Why is that strange little girl .... me? I don't know her!
   a staring at   **b** avoiding making eye contact with
10 'Try not to .... while I'm doing the eye examination,' said the doctor.
   a rub your eyes   **b** blink

READING

1 Read the article on page 61 quickly. Choose the best title.

a Why lying is bad for you
b How to lie effectively
c Lying – the good news and the bad news

2 Read the article again. Put the sub-headings in the correct place.

1 How to spot one
2 Everybody's doing it!
3 The bad
4 Starting early
5 The good

Let's be honest: you've told some little white lies, haven't you? Maybe you told your sister her new dress looked great when you really thought it was horrible. Perhaps you told your teacher you left your homework on the kitchen table when the truth was you forgot to do it. Or maybe you told your friend that you couldn't go out because you were busy when in fact you just didn't want to go out.

A ....

Don't feel too bad about it. You're not alone! Research shows that people lie all the time. In fact, even the most honest of us do it at least once a day. Scientists have suggested lying might be necessary for society to work properly – and, in some cases, it might even be good for you.

B ....

We learn how to lie at a very young age. Our first experiments with lying happen at around the age of three. Just a few years later, we're pretty good at it – and do it several times a day. It is believed that children learn to lie by observing their parents do it. Sometimes, parents even encourage children to lie – it's often just a case of teaching good manners: 'Thank you for my present. I love it!' and 'That was delicious.' are two common examples.

C ....

There are many other reasons why we tell lies, apart from politeness. Maybe we want to get some kind of reward or advantage, for example, or maybe we want to protect someone from getting their feelings hurt. We even lie to ourselves, which can have some positive effects. People who boast about their abilities in something – even if those abilities are not so great – often improve faster than those who are more realistic in their self-assessment.

D ....

But of course, it's not all good news. If you're deceiving yourself to an unrealistic level, it can have a damaging effect on your confidence when you fail. If your innocent and polite lies to others are discovered, that can have a terrible effect on your relationships because you will no longer be trusted. Even if your little white lie is not discovered, knowing that you've told it can damage your own self-image as a good and honest person, making you feel bad.

E ....

So how can you tell if someone is lying to you? It depends on how big the lie is. Little white lies, such as 'That was a lovely meal,' are hard to detect, because they're easy to tell. But when someone tells a serious lie, especially if they aren't used to lying, their heart rate and body temperature may increase. They may also appear very nervous.

To sum up, there are both positive and negative things about lying. Ultimately, the little lies we tell every day probably do more good than harm, provided they are told well enough not to make anyone suspicious. Big lies, on the other hand, should be avoided. Although they may produce advantages in the short term, the damage they do to your sense of self-worth is a high price to pay. And that price gets much higher if you develop the reputation of being a liar!

3 **Match the statements to the paragraphs A–E.**

Which paragraph
1 gives an example of how lying can help us improve? ....
2 informs us that lying is common? ....
3 lists some bad consequences of lying? ....
4 compares some kinds of lying with being polite? ....
5 looks at two kinds of lying and their effect on us? ....

4 **Find words in the text which mean the following.**

1 watching (paragraph B) ....
2 something that will help you succeed (paragraph C) ....
3 imaginary, or very far from the actual truth (paragraph D) ....
4 not trusting someone or something (conclusion) ....
5 the opinion of someone based on their behaviour or character in the past (conclusion) ....

EP Word profile *matter*

Complete the sentences with the words in the box.

| educational   fact   knowledge |
| the fact   what |

1 In .... matters, our head teacher is an expert.
2 As a matter of .... , this is my first time in France.
3 She always tells the truth, no matter .... anyone says.
4 .... of the matter is, there is no money left in your bank account.
5 I'm afraid I don't have any .... of the matter.

GRAMMAR *have/get something done;*
get someone to do something

1 **Complete the sentences with the correct form of the verbs in the box.**

> bring   cut   feed   fix   install
> publish   steal   test

1 I got my uncle .... my broken bike wheel – he's good at things like that.
2 Mum had her car .... when she left it at the station overnight.
3 What time are you getting your hair .... this afternoon?
4 He was very happy when he had his letter .... in the local newspaper.
5 We're going to get our neighbour .... our fish while we're on holiday.
6 My rich aunt likes to have her breakfast .... to her room when she stays in a hotel.
7 That referee should have his eyes ....!
8 We got a new bathroom .... in our house last month.

2 **Write the words in the correct order to make sentences.**

1 broken / our front window / had / last night / We
   ....
   ....

2 got / The teacher / to tidy / after school / the classroom / the students
   ....
   ....

3 in an accident / Steven / his arm / broken / had
   ....
   ....

4 a doctor / should / to check / You / your eyes / get
   ....
   ....

5 got / We / painted / last week / our living room
   ....
   ....

6 in my project / getting / my spelling / my dad / I'm / to check
   ....
   ....

7 had / bright blue! / her fingernails / painted / has / Pilar
   ....
   ....

8 load the dishwasher / us / Mum / gets / to / after breakfast / always
   ....
   ....

3 **Answer the questions.**

1 Does she cut her hair herself?
   No, she .... at a hairdresser's.
2 Did you wrap all those presents yourself?
   No, I .... for me.
3 Is Tim going to design his own webpage?
   No, he .... it for him.
4 Do you fix your own bike?
   No, I .... at the bike shop.
5 Is Tina going to make her own wedding dress?
   No, she .... by a professional.
6 Do you iron your own clothes?
   No, I .... for me.

4 ⊙ **Choose the correct sentence in each pair.**

1 a The car is a safe means of transportation if you have your seat belt fasten.
   b The car is a safe means of transportation if you have your seat belt fastened.
2 a She took me to the hospital, where the doctor told me that I had my leg broken.
   b She took me to the hospital, where the doctor told me that I had broken my leg.
3 a I prefer working with the animals, but I know how hard it is to get someone to help in the office.
   b I prefer working with the animals, but I know how hard it is to get someone to helping in the office.
4 a I took her by her shoulders for her to stop yelling for a while.
   b I took her by her shoulders to get her to stop yelling for a while.
5 a A car is quite expensive and it costs money every time you get it repaired.
   b A car is quite expensive and it costs money every time you get it to be repaired.
6 a You can make more people to take part by holding swimming competitions.
   b You can get more people to take part by holding swimming competitions.

VOCABULARY   -self, -selves for emphasis

1 **Choose the correct answer.**

1 We had to fix our flat tyre *itself / ourselves*.

2 That day, Daniel and Ellie met the president *himself / ourselves*.

3 My grandparents built this house *myself / themselves*.

4 Stephanie makes all her clothes *herself / themselves*.

5 I will finish this project *itself / myself*.

6 Tidy your room *himself / yourself*, you lazy boy.

7 We didn't get to see the Eiffel Tower *ourselves / itself* – just a model of it.

8 Did you and your brother decorate this whole room *itself / yourselves*?

2 **Match the sentences 1–6 to the replies a–f.**

1 Who cooked dinner for you?   ....

2 Make me a sandwich.   ....

3 Who tidied your brothers' room?   ....

4 Nobody is going to help us.   ....

5 Sally looks such a mess.   ....

6 It was an interesting exhibition.   ....

a She shouldn't cut her hair herself.

b I met the photographer himself afterwards.

c Do it yourself.

d I did it myself.

e They did it themselves.

f We have to do it ourselves.

WRITING   Expressing opinions
See Prepare to write box, Student's Book page 13.

1 **Look at these titles. Match them with sentences 1–6 below. (There are three sentences for each title.)**

a It is always wrong to tell a lie.

b Cars should be banned from city centres.

c Children under 12 should not be allowed to use social media.

1 <u>There is no doubt that</u> pollution is a problem.   ....

2 <u>It is often said that</u> the truth sometimes hurts.   ....

3 <u>I believe that</u> writing standards have actually improved.   ....

4 <u>In my opinion</u>, shops would do more business, not less.   ....

5 <u>It is obvious that</u> face-to-face communication is essential for true understanding.   ....

6 <u>Some people think that</u> other people's feelings are the most important thing.   ....

7 <u>As far as I'm concerned</u>, though, we should try our best to be truthful at all times.   ....

8 <u>It is generally felt that</u> shorter journeys could more often be done on foot.   ....

9 <u>Personally, I think</u> it's a matter of supervising their use of phones and tablets.   ....

2 **Look at the introductory parts of the sentences in exercise 1 (underlined). Which ones give a personal opinion? Which ones give a general opinion? Complete the table.**

Personal opinion	General opinion

3 **Look at this first paragraph. Which title is it for? Rewrite it using correct punctuation.**

most of us were taught from an early age that lying is wrong but is this always true are there some circumstances when it would be better to tell a lie i think so and i will try to explain why

....

....

....

....

....

....

4 **Think of three or four arguments for and against lying. (You can use the article on page 61.) Make notes in the table below. Think of examples of the different kinds of lie.**

Lying is bad …	Lying is not bad …
Example:	Example:

5 **Now decide which of the notes in the table express your opinion and which are more general. Write them with suitable introductory expressions from exercise 2.**

....

....

....

....

....

....

....

....

6 **Now choose one of the other titles from exercise 1. Make some notes about it to express your opinion and general opinion. Write the opinions in full sentences with suitable introductory expressions.**

16 Who cares?

VOCABULARY Climate change

1 Complete the puzzle using the clues below.

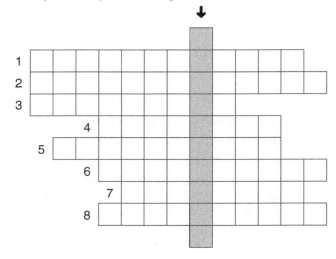

1 the protection of nature
2 the gas formed when people or animals breathe out (two words)
3 when paper, glass, plastic, etc. is put through a process so that it can be used again
4 this produces energy from the movement of air (two words)
5 energy produced by the sun (two words)
6 the production of energy in a particular form
7 if something is environmentally-....... , it doesn't harm the environment
8 the mixture of gases around the Earth
↓ a type of landscape that has suffered a lot of destruction

2 Choose the correct words to complete the text.

We've just had a lesson on climate change at school. Mr Green explained all about the problem of producing too much [1] *solar power / carbon dioxide* and what it is doing to the [2] *atmosphere / recycling*.

'Firstly, we need to prevent the total destruction of the [3] *conservation / rainforests* because trees breathe in CO_2 and produce the oxygen,' he said. 'We also need to find more [4] *environmentally-friendly / recycling* ways to produce energy.'

Mr Green showed us a picture of a [5] *solar power / wind farm*, and we all made a promise to try to do more [6] *recycling / generation*.

It was a great lesson!

3 Complete the sentences with words from exercise 1.

1 We need to find ways to encourage the .... of empty bottles and newspapers.
2 The .... of natural habitats is very important for the future of the Earth.
3 The South American .... has suffered a lot of destruction.
4 .... and .... are very cheap and environmentally-friendly methods for the .... of electricity.
5 Too much .... is being released into the .... , which is causing climate change.

READING

1 Read the first two paragraphs of the article. Think of the word which best fits each gap.

Six surprising results of climate change

Most people have a general idea **(0)** .... *about* .... what global warming involves. The data showing rising temperatures and melting ice caps is there **(1)** .... all to see, and rising sea levels **(2)** .... predicted to happen in the near future. But the Earth's changing climate is already causing problems.

1

Not **(3)** .... is global warming melting glaciers and creating more powerful hurricanes, but it also seems to be causing more forest fires **(4)** .... ever before. **(5)** .... is more, recent wildfires in the western USA have both covered larger areas and lasted for longer. Their increased size and frequency mean that fire fighters have a much harder time putting them **(6)** .... There is a clear relationship **(7)** .... the warmer temperatures and the early arrival of spring. When the snow disappears, forest areas become drier and stay dry for longer, **(8)** .... increases the chance that they might catch fire.

2 Match the pictures on page 65 to the rest of the paragraphs.

2 Photo ....

All over the world, temples, ancient monuments and other statues stand as reminders of civilisations past, which until now have survived the tests of time. However the immediate effects of global warming may finally destroy them. Rising seas and extreme weather have the potential to damage these unique sites. Floods caused by global warming have already damaged Sukhathai – the 600-year-old site which was the ancient capital of a Thai kingdom.

3 Photo ....

The average climber probably wouldn't notice, but the Alps and other mountain ranges have experienced gradual growth over the past century or so thanks to the melting of the glaciers on top of them. For thousands of years, the weight of these glaciers has pushed the mountains down into the earth, squeezing it down like a cushion. As the glaciers melt, this weight is decreasing, and the surface is slowly rising. Global warming speeds up the melting of these glaciers, so the mountains are growing faster!

4 Photo ....

One hundred and twenty-five lakes in the Arctic have disappeared in the past few decades, giving support to the idea that global warming is working extremely fast nearest the Earth's poles. Research into the missing water points to the probability that frozen earth underneath the lakes warmed up and became soft – or thawed. As this normally permanently-frozen ground thaws, the water in the lakes can escape through the soil, draining the lake. One researcher compared it to pulling the plug out of the bath.

5 Photo ....

While melting ice in the Arctic might cause problems for plants and animals further south, it's creating a bright and sunny situation for Arctic vegetation. Arctic plants are usually trapped in ice for most of the year. Now in spring, when the ice melts earlier, the plants start growing quickly. There has been an explosion of plant growth in the Arctic in the past decades!

6 Photo ....

Have those itchy eyes and sneezing fits that bother you every spring got worse in recent years? Global warming may be partly to blame for that, too. Over the past few decades, an increasing number of people have started suffering from seasonal allergies and asthma. Just like in the Arctic, early springs mean plants come into flower more quickly, so your allergy season can last longer. Better buy some more tissues!

3 Answer the questions about the text.

1 Why do early springs make forest fires more likely?
....
....

2 What caused the damage to an ancient site in Thailand?
....
....

3 Why are mountains getting higher?
....
....

4 What is the cause of the 'explosion of plant growth' in the Arctic?
....
....

5 How does climate change affect people with allergies?
....
....

EP Word profile *set*

Choose the correct answers.

1 The prisoner was set *free* / *out* the next morning.
2 Have you set a *date* / *record* for the spelling test?
3 I'm trying to set *off* / *up* a meeting for the ecology club.
4 Please try to set a good *time* / *example* for your younger sister.
5 What time are you setting *up* / *off* tomorrow morning?
6 The athlete is trying to set a new *example* / *record*.
7 I've set *out* / *off* all the important details in this file.
8 My uncle has just set *out* / *up* his own business.
9 I'm setting the *record* / *alarm* for 6.30 tomorrow morning.
10 Where is the new *film* / *target* about climate change set?
11 We set *out* / *up* on our journey on Saturday morning.
12 The new *school* / *time* is set on the east side of the city.

GRAMMAR Second conditional: *would, could* and *might; I wish* and *if only*

1 Match the beginnings and endings of the sentences.

1 I'd tour the world on a bicycle ....
2 If I was rich, ...
3 I could help you with your project ....
4 If I wasn't busy this weekend, ...
5 I wouldn't go to school every day ....
6 If recycling wasn't so important, ...

a I'd buy an electric car.
b if I had enough money.
c if you wanted me to.
d I might go to the cinema.
e I wouldn't do it.
f if I didn't have to.

2 Complete the sentences with the verbs in the second conditional. Use *could* or *might* if possible.

1 If we .... (recycle) more glass and paper, we .... (save) more energy.
2 The kids .... (go) outside if the weather .... (not be) so bad.
3 You .... (do) better in your exams if you .... (work) a bit harder.
4 He .... (write) to her if he .... (know) her email address.
5 If we .... (not have) to go to school today, we .... (go) to the beach.
6 If she .... (stop) using her tablet an hour before going to bed, she .... (sleep) better.
7 We .... (be) lost if we .... (not have) our mobile phones with us.
8 Global warming .... (be) slowed if all the governments in the world .... (make) an effort.
9 It .... (be) much easier to recycle all our rubbish if we .... (have) different bins for everything.
10 If I .... (work) every Saturday morning from now to my exams, I .... (be) able to go on holiday with my friends in the summer.
11 If Maria .... (smile) and .... (chat) a bit more with people, she .... (make) more friends.
12 Mum and Dad say we .... (save) a lot of money if my brother and I .... (turn) off the lights more often!

3 Complete the sentences with the correct words from the box.

be / rich   be / sunny   can / get to sleep
~~have / an umbrella~~   not be / closed
not play / loud music   speak / Chinese

0 It's pouring down. I wish ....I had an umbrella.....
1 I'd love a Ferrari. If only ....
2 I'm so worried about the test tomorrow. If only ....
3 We'd love to go to the beach today. If only ....
4 Oh, I'm too late to get the shopping. I wish ....
5 I don't understand a word on this holiday. I wish ....
6 These new neighbours are nice, but I wish ....

4 👁 Correct the mistakes in these sentences or put a tick (✔) by any you think are correct.

1 If everyone pays, it might be cheaper.
....
2 I would be grateful if you correct your errors.
....
3 I wish you will send me the answers.
....
4 I tried to persuade him that there was no danger, and if anything happened he could wake me up.
....
5 There's not a lot for young people to do, so it could be good if you invented something!
....

VOCABULARY Conditional phrases

Choose the correct answer.

1 *Assuming / Even if* more wind farms are built in the next few years, electricity should get cheaper.
2 She wouldn't invite him to her party *assuming / even if* he asked her.
3 I'll buy some new trainers *as long as / even if* they aren't too expensive.
4 You may go to the pool without an adult *provided that / even if* you are over 14 years old.
5 *As long as / Even if* we had enough oil to last another 100 years, we should still try to find alternative forms of energy.
6 You'll save a lot of electricity *as long as / even if* you follow the recommendations in this article.

LISTENING

1 **What are the advantages and disadvantages of wind farms? Make a list in the table below.**

Advantages	Disadvantages

2 ▶10 **You will hear a girl called Samantha talking about a trip to a wind farm. Does she mention any of the things you put in the table? Tick (✔) them.**

3 ▶10 **Listen again and complete the sentences with a word or short phrase.**

1 Samantha says that the people in the village were most worried about the .... of the proposed wind farm.
2 The trip was organised by the .... at Samantha's school.
3 There were .... people who went on the trip to visit the wind farm.
4 One of the visitors used the word .... to describe the wind farm.
5 Samantha reports that the visit to the wind farm ended because of ....
6 Samantha says that .... of the wind farm was what especially impressed the visitors.
7 After the visit, the only thing people were still worried about was the .... of the turbines.
8 Samantha uses the example of a .... to explain why the turbines have to be tall.
9 Samantha explains that the reason turbines are so tall is because the .... is greater up there.
10 Samantha points out that we need to use more .... for generating electricity.

4 **Complete the conversation with the phrases below.**

a I agree with you up to a point
b there are various pros and cons
c Another thing is
d the main advantage is that
e overall
f For a start

A: What do you think about wind farms?
B: Well, obviously, [1] .... For me, [2] .... they provide almost free energy! What do you think?
A: I don't like them at all for a number of reasons. [3] .... , they're really ugly.
B: That's a matter of opinion. I think they're quite beautiful.
A: [4] .... that they're unreliable. No wind, no energy!
B: [5] .... – they aren't a complete solution to our energy problems. But I think [6] .... they can make an important contribution, when combined with solar power and other forms of electricity generation.
A: Yeah, you're probably right.

5 ▶11 **Listen to the conversation and check your answers.**

a wind turbine

a wind farm

17 Art is fun!

VOCABULARY Adjectives describing art

1 Complete the adjectives with the correct vowels.

1 C L ....S S C
2 C ....N T R ....V ....R S L
3 B ....Z ....R R ....
4 D R ....M ....T C
5 ....M P R ....S S ....V ....
6 M Y S T ....R ....S

7 C ....M P L X
8 M ....S S ....V ....
9 ....N .... Q ....
10 ....B S T R ....C T
11 C ....N T ....M P ....R ....R Y
12 C ....N V ....N T ....N L

2 Now write the adjectives in exercise 1 next to their meanings.

a very sudden or noticeable, or full of action and excitement ....
b very large in size, amount or number ....
c popular for a long time and considered to be of a high quality ....
d strange or unknown, and not explained or understood ....
e very strange and unusual ....
f different from everyone and everything else ....
g complicated and difficult to understand ....
h existing or happening now ....
i causing disagreement or discussion ....
j causing admiration and respect ....
k (of art) involving shapes and colours and not images of real things or people ....
l traditional and ordinary ....

3 Choose the correct answers.

1 I don't really like .... art – I prefer to look at pictures of real things.
   a massive   **b** abstract   **c** impressive
2 He's a very .... artist, whose work makes some people angry.
   a controversial   **b** classic   **c** dramatic
3 The painting was so .... it covered the whole wall.
   a unique   **b** mysterious   **c** massive
4 Do you prefer .... art, or older more traditional paintings?
   a classic   **b** contemporary   **c** complex
5 Nobody else paints like this artist – her work is ....
   a dramatic   **b** mysterious   **c** unique
6 His work is not very interesting or adventurous – in fact, it is boringly ....
   a massive   **b** conventional   **c** dramatic
7 This style of art is much too .... for me to understand.
   a controversial   **b** classic   **c** complex
8 For a first attempt at this style, your painting is very .... – well done!
   a impressive   **b** conventional   **c** abstract

READING

1 Look at the example of graffiti art on page 69. What makes it different from more traditional forms of art?

....
....

2 Read the first paragraph of the article below, about a graffiti artist called Banksy. Decide which answer (A, B, C or D) best fits each gap.

0	**A** displayed	**B** appeared	**C** designed	**D** presented
1	**A** discover	**B** encounter	**C** meet	**D** gain
2	**A** begun	**B** tended	**C** become	**D** developed
3	**A** said	**B** claimed	**C** promised	**D** admitted
4	**A** honest	**B** responsible	**C** steady	**D** reliable
5	**A** got	**B** solved	**C** won	**D** reached
6	**A** found	**B** looked	**C** obtained	**D** searched
7	**A** occupation	**B** function	**C** job	**D** work
8	**A** introduced	**B** responded	**C** identified	**D** connected

Graffiti art by Banksy

BANKSY, WHO ARE YOU?

For years, his artwork has mysteriously **(0)** ...B.. on walls and buildings across the world. But nobody knows who he is. Indeed, the ten-year mission to **(1)** .... the true identity of the graffiti artist known as 'Banksy' has **(2)** .... almost as fascinating as the controversial artwork itself. While many people have **(3)** .... to know who he is, the only **(4)** .... facts are that he comes from Bristol and his first name is Robin. Now the mystery may have been **(5)** .... A national newspaper says it **(6)** .... out the name of the artist using a photograph which apparently showed him at **(7)** .... with spray cans in Jamaica in 2004. The newspaper contacted several of his friends, who all **(8)** .... the man in the picture as Robin Gunningham, an ex-pupil from an expensive private school in Bristol.

Yesterday the artist's agents refused to confirm whether Mr Gunningham was actually Banksy. 'We get these calls all the time,' said his spokeswoman. 'I never confirm or deny these stories.'

Since Banksy became a major street artist, his work has sold for thousands of pounds. Last year, a piece of his controversial graffiti which was painted on a London wall sold for over £200,000 in an online auction. People who have bought Banksy artwork include the actor Angelina Jolie and the singer Christina Aguilera. He's certainly fashionable!

His journey to fame is an unusual one. One of the first conventional exhibitions of his art was held in 2000, but the mysterious Banksy gave out only the number of the building and not the name of the street. Nevertheless, interest in him began to grow. He developed strategies to keep his identity secret, such as doing interviews only on the phone and using trusted business colleagues to handle sales.

As his fame grew, so did the danger of being caught spraying his unique graffiti on public walls. He began to think up more complex and unusual stunts. For example, he got into the penguin exhibit at the London Zoo and painted 'We're bored of fish' on the wall. Then in October 2003 he hung one of his own paintings in the famous Tate Gallery in London. It showed a country scene surrounded by police tape. He did a similar thing in 2005 at four major museums in New York City. One of those museums – the Museum of Modern Art – decided to add the piece to their permanent collection!

When Banksy does agree to give an interview, he ensures that the public never discover his true identity. 'I have no interest in ever coming out,' he told an arts magazine. 'I'm just trying to make the pictures look good; I'm not into trying to make myself look good. And besides, it's a pretty safe bet that the reality of me would be a crushing disappointment to a couple of 15-year-old kids out there.'

Maybe now that it looks like his identity has finally been revealed, that may well change.

3 Read the rest of the article. According to the writer, are the following statements true (T) or false (F), or is the information not given (NG)?

1 Banksy's managers frequently deal with enquiries about his identity. ....

2 Very few people turned up to Banksy's first exhibition. ....

3 Banksy does not care about being caught. ....

4 Banksy employs people to look after the business side of his art. ....

5 A museum in the USA kept one of Banksy's paintings to display to visitors. ....

6 Banksy says that he will one day reveal his identity to the world. ....

EP **Word profile** *scale*

Complete the sentences with the words below.

one to ten	problem	smaller	to

1 We still don't know the scale of the ....

2 On a scale of .... , I'd give it three.

3 This model of my house isn't .... scale.

4 These plans are similar to the previous ones, but on a .... scale.

GRAMMAR Modals of deduction: Present

1 Complete the sentences with *must* or *can't*.

1 Look at all those football trophies. She .... be a really good player.

2 She isn't answering the door. She .... be at home.

3 He has a strong Spanish accent. He .... be from Spain.

4 You've just had lunch. You .... be hungry!

5 They haven't had a drink all afternoon. They .... be thirsty.

6 He drives a Ferrari. He .... be rich.

7 Nobody is buying her cakes. They .... taste very nice.

8 She's got a lot of books. She .... love reading.

2 Chose the correct modal verbs.

1 Dan and Michael .... be in the same class, but I'm not sure.
   a can't   **b** must   **c** could

2 That .... be Amanda in the shop. She's on holiday.
   a can't   **b** must   **c** could

3 You .... be right – you often are.
   a can't   **b** might well   **c** must

4 We .... come back to Florida next year, as we've had such a good time.
   a might well   **b** can well   **c** can't

5 This .... be the first time you've seen this film – it's been out for ages!
   a could   **b** must   **c** can't

6 The shops .... be closed by now. What time do they close on Thursdays?
   a can't   **b** could   **c** must

3 Complete the sentences using the words in brackets.

1 I'm sure my keys are in this room somewhere! (must)
   My keys ....

2 Sonja definitely isn't from France. (can't)
   Sonja ....

3 It seems quite likely that it will rain later. (well)
   It ....

4 I'm not sure if Tom is going to win this race. (lose)
   Tom ....

5 Jane is in Mexico, so I'm certain that isn't her on the bus. (be)
   That ....

6 Surely you aren't serious about wanting to be an astronaut. (joking)
   You ....

4 ⊙ Correct the mistakes in these sentences or put a tick (✔) by any you think are correct.

1 Both talks must be very interesting.
   ....

2 It could be difficult for me. ....

3 She thinks that the computer takes too much time and that it can be harmful for my health.
   ....

4 It mustn't be very nice for the animals to be disturbed all day and to have no freedom.
   ....

5 You must be the tourists from England.
   ....

VOCABULARY Verb meanings often in the passive

1 Choose the correct passive verbs.

1 The president of our club was .... last year.
   a influenced   **b** elected   **c** prohibited

2 When was this university .... ?
   a established **b** awarded   **c** devoted

3 The entire first floor of the building was .... to the art exhibition.
   a elected   **b** set   **c** devoted

4 I was .... by my father in my decision to study music.
   a influenced   **b** composed   **c** regarded

5 Our team was .... a silver medal in the volleyball tournament.
   a elected   **b** awarded   **c** entitled

2 Rewrite the sentences using the passive form of the verbs below.

> award   compose   entitle
> prohibit   regard   set

0 The school gave Maria a prize for her work with younger pupils.
   ...Maria was awarded a prize for her ....
   ...work with younger pupils...........................

1 They don't allow ball games in this park.
   ....
   ....

2 A tiny island is the location for this novel.
   ....
   ....

3 People think Banksy is a good artist.
   ....
   ....

4 *Art in the City* is the name of the TV programme.
   ....
   ....

5 The final concert consisted of five bands, each doing half an hour.
   ....
   ....

WRITING An essay

See Prepare to write box, Student's Book page 101.

1 Read the essay title. Write two points for 1 and 2 in the Notes section. Add your own idea.

> **Art is not a subject which should be taught in schools. Do you agree?**
>
> **Notes**
> Write about:
> ....
> ....
> ....
>
> **1** the value of art
> **2** the purpose of education
> **3** .... (your own idea)

2 Read the essay quickly. Are your points included?

3 Read the essay again and number the paragraphs in the correct order.

1 .... (introduction)
2 .... (points against the title)
3 .... (points for the title)
4 .... (conclusion)

A On the other hand, art is regarded by most people as an important part of life. It helps us to understand the world. Therefore it should be included in the education system. What is more, artists can create wealth by selling their works, so it is not a complete waste of time. For example, Banksy is very rich and he attracts visitors to the country.

B Some people would argue that art is not a necessary subject. They may believe that the purpose of education is to produce people who can create wealth for the country by helping businesses to grow and making useful things. To these people, art is just a waste of time.

C In my view art is a very important part of human culture. I believe that it should always be taught in schools.

D This is a very controversial question. Nearly all schools teach art to their students, but are there any reasons why they should not?

4 Read the essay again and find the points for and against the title. Underline the points for in one colour and the points against in another colour.

5 Match the highlighted words and expressions to the following alternatives.

1 I think ....
2 Some might say ....
3 For this reason, ...
4 For instance, ...
5 In contrast, ...
6 In my opinion, ...
7 Furthermore, ...

6 Read the essay title. Write two points for 1 and 2 in the Notes section and add your own idea. Label each one *for* or *against*.

> **Graffiti is not art, it is a crime. Do you agree?**
>
> **Notes**
> Write about:
> ....
> ....
> ....
>
> **1** why graffiti is prohibited
> **2** positive things about graffiti
> **3** .... (your own idea)

7 Write your essay in 140–180 words. Use the plan in exercise 3 and some of the linking words in exercise 5.

VOCABULARY Nouns: personal qualities

1 Complete the crossword using the clues below.

Across

1 someone's/something's ability to develop, achieve or succeed
5 enthusiasm for doing something
6 the ability to deal with a dangerous or difficult situation without being frightened
8 an enthusiastic and determined attitude
9 when someone continues trying to do something, although it is very difficult
10 the quality of being sincere and telling the truth

Down

2 someone/something that gives you ideas for doing something
3 willingness to give your time and energy to something, or a promise to do something
4 the state of being happy to do something if it is needed
7 the noun related to *brave*

2 Choose the correct answers. Sometimes two are correct.

1 I admire your *motivation / honesty / potential* – not many people would admit to something like that.
2 You have the *spirit / inspiration / potential* to succeed, if you are willing to try.
3 There's a lack of *motivation / spirit / honesty* in the team, which means it is unlikely to win anything this season.
4 I haven't got the *honesty / inspiration / commitment* to be a top athlete.
5 It took a lot of *courage / potential / bravery* to get up on stage and speak to the crowd like that.
6 My father was my *determination / willingness / inspiration* to take up singing seriously.

3 Complete the sentences with words from exercise 1. Sometimes more than one word is possible.

1 It takes a lot of .... to complete a marathon, as it is so easy to give up before the end.
2 My grandfather was given a medal for his .... during the war.
3 We were all impressed by Susanna's .... to help around the house.
4 Usain Bolt is a real .... to many young athletes.
5 I think Sandra has the .... to become a good leader – she just needs to try a bit harder.
6 My .... to train every day decreased as the weather got hotter.
7 There's a really good team .... among our football players.

READING

1 Read the article on page 73 quickly. Where do you think it comes from?

a a textbook
b an internet magazine
c a newspaper

2 Read the article again. Match the titles to the paragraphs.

1 Keep moving!   ....
2 Value your friendships   ....
3 Work hard at school   ....
4 Behave yourself!   ....
5 Enjoy life   ....
6 Get involved in your community   ....
7 Be nice to your parents and teacher   ....
8 Find out what you want to do in life   ....

3 Find at least one reason for doing each of the following when you're a teen.

Why should you

1 volunteer?

....

2 start thinking about work?

....

3 be nice to parents and teachers?

....

4 make sure you keep active?

....

5 take all the opportunities you can?

....

EIGHT STEPS to SUCCESS
in the teen years

If you want to be successful in life, it's a good idea to start young. Follow these eight steps, and success will come your way.

A Boring!!! Yawn!!! Maybe, but a good education will help you succeed in later life. Do the best you possibly can: listen to your teachers, study hard for tests, always do your homework. If you want a great job in the future, this is your first step.

B Be a volunteer! That's really cool these days, and everyone knows that doing things for others makes you happy. Whether you work with old people or animals, or help keep the local area clean and free from litter, you're making the world a better place. And it's good experience to tell a future employer!

C It may seem like ages away from now, but work is really just around the corner. Now is a good time to start thinking about what kind of career you want to end up in. The sooner you have an idea about what your goals are, the sooner you can make the decisions now that will help you achieve them.

D Getting into trouble now could have a really bad effect on your future prospects. This isn't the easiest time to avoid dangerous, unhealthy activities, because you have so much energy and a need to explore. But don't worry – it gets easier as you get older!

E Yes, we all know how difficult they can be, but they're there to help you, and they do have your best interests at heart. They deserve your respect. It's not always easy, but think of it as good practice for when you've got an irritating boss!

F Some say your friends are the most important people in your life. So choose them well! Stay close to the people who make you laugh and make you feel loved, and be there for them when they need you. Some of the friends you make now will be with you for the rest of your life.

G Whether you join a sports team, take up cycling, go swimming, or just walk – make sure you exercise. You'll feel better mentally and physically. We know that active teens are more likely to become and stay active adults, which inevitably leads to a longer, healthier and happier life.

H You're only young once, and before long you'll be an adult with a full-time job and other responsibilities. Make sure you won't regret all the things you didn't do when you were a teenager. Be bold! Take risks! Make the most of your teen years!

4 Find words in the text with these meanings.

1 a person who does something to help, without getting paid (paragraph B) ....
2 the possibility of being successful (paragraph D) ....
3 annoying (paragraph E) ....
4 connected with or related to the mind (paragraph G) ....
5 not frightened of taking risks (paragraph H) ....

EP Word profile *face*

Match the use of *face* in the sentences to the meanings below. (Two have the same meaning.)

1 I had to face many difficulties as a teenager, but I'm quite successful now. ......
2 The look on my brother's face was unforgettable! ......
3 You'll just have to face up to the fact that you aren't very good at maths. ......
4 I couldn't face telling Mum that I'd failed the exam. ......
5 Why don't you face the truth? We can't afford to go on holiday this year. ......

a not want to do something unpleasant
b the front part of the head
c deal with or overcome a problem
d accept that a difficult situation exists

GRAMMAR   Third conditional; *wish* + past perfect

1 Choose the correct verb forms.

1 We *might enjoy / might have enjoyed* the meal if the waiter hadn't been so rude.

2 If you *understand / had understood* the question, you might have given the right answer.

3 They would have been very cold if they *didn't take / hadn't taken* their coats.

4 Maria *will visit / would have visited* more places if she had had enough time.

5 If the acting *was / had been* better, that could have been a great film.

6 If Simon *didn't get up / hadn't got up* so late, he might not have missed the bus.

7 You *wouldn't meet / wouldn't have met* your favourite actor if you hadn't gone to the theatre that evening.

8 If Mum and Dad *didn't sell / hadn't sold* our car, we might not have been able to afford a holiday.

2 Rewrite the sentences using the third conditional. Use *might* or *could* if possible.

0 She didn't tell me the time of her train, so I didn't go to meet her.
If *she had told me the time of her train, I would have gone to meet her.*

1 I didn't have lunch because I wasn't hungry.
I ....

2 You told him it was a great book, so he bought it.
If ....

3 He failed the test because he hadn't studied.
He ....

4 Steve didn't hear about the party, so he didn't go.
If ....

5 I had drunk all the milk, so Mum couldn't make a cheese sauce.
Mum ....

6 Your bag was stolen because you left it outside.
If ....

7 I started a new school last year and met my best friend.
If ....

8 You were rude to Irina yesterday so it isn't surprising she ignored you today!
Irina ....

3 Complete the sentences with *I wish* and a verb from the box in the correct form.

book	not crash	not eat	not go
have	know	phone	not spend
not stop	~~study~~	wear	

0 ....*I wish I had studied*........ harder at school.

1 .... to bed so late last night.

2 .... about Matt's party.

3 .... tickets for the Haim concert.

4 .... so much chocolate.

5 .... a warmer coat.

6 .... all my money on these new trainers.

7 .... you earlier today.

8 .... learning to play the piano.

9 .... my bicycle into the wall yesterday.

10 .... the courage to say what I thought.

4 ◉ Correct the mistakes in these sentences or put a tick (✔) by any you think are correct.

1 If we had took the plane, we wouldn't have seen so many interesting places. ....

2 If you have been there, you would enjoyed yourself! ....

3 Finally, I'd like to tell you that if I had known it, I would have stayed at your home for the rest of my holiday. ....

4 I think many problems going to appear if I had bought it. ....

5 I really wish you were here with me last month. ....

6 I liked it very much and I wish you would have been able to go with me. ....

VOCABULARY   Phrasal verbs with *get*

1 Match the verbs to their meanings.

1 get away with ....
2 get back ....
3 get into ....
4 get on with ....
5 get out of ....
6 get round to ....
7 get through ....

a avoid doing something that you don't want to do, especially by giving an excuse

b be given something again that you had before

c do something that you have intended to do for a long time

d succeed in not being criticised or punished for something

e succeed in e.g. an examination or competition

f continue doing something, especially work

g be chosen or elected, e.g. for a team

2 Choose the correct answers.

1 Our football team has got .... to the semi-finals.
   a through   **b** back   **c** round

2 Don't lend any money to John, or you'll never get it ....
   a out   **b** back   **c** away

3 I thought I'd got .... with forgetting my homework, but the teacher remembered to ask me for it.
   a out   **b** through   **c** away

4 We've finally got .... to painting my bedroom!
   a round   **b** off   **c** through

5 I'm staying in tonight to get .... with my project.
   a on   **b** away   **c** out

6 Carmen was very happy to learn she had got .... her chosen university.
   a away   **b** through   **c** into

7 The only way you can get .... of washing the dishes is if you cook the dinner!
   a out   **b** away   **c** round

LISTENING

1 You will hear an interview with a backgammon player called Shani Okello. Look at the photos and read through the questions quickly. What do you think Shani's story is?

2 ▶12 Look at the questions or start of sentences on the right (i.e. the first lines). Listen and make notes of the answers. Check your answers to exercise 1.

1 ....
2 ....
3 ....
4 ....
5 ....
6 ....
7 ....

3 ▶12 Listen to the interview with Shani again and choose the best answer (A, B or C).

1 When Shani first saw backgammon, she was attracted to it because
   A it looked like a quiet and peaceful game.
   B the children seemed to be enjoying it.
   C it got her off the streets.

2 Shani lost her first few games because
   A she didn't know how to plan.
   B she was having too much fun.
   C she was too impatient.

3 What does Shani particularly like about backgammon?
   A It is similar to real life.
   B It helps her forget her problems.
   C There is no luck involved in it.

4 Shani believes the most important quality in a backgammon player is
   A determination.
   B mathematical skill.
   C honesty.

5 What excuse does Shani give for her poor performance in Siberia?
   A She was tired from the travelling.
   B The weather was very bad.
   C She lacked experience.

6 Shani is impatient with backgammon players who
   A don't study enough.
   B try too hard to become champions.
   C blame the dice when they lose.

7 Shani says that backgammon has
   A made her wealthy.
   B improved her future prospects.
   C allowed her to make new friends.

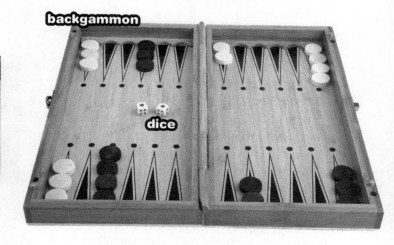

backgammon

dice

VOCABULARY Crime and criminals

1 Write the words and phrases below in the correct column.

burgle	hacker	statement
burglar	investigate	suspect
burglary	judge	theft
charge	jury	victim
commit a crime	make an arrest	witness
court	release	
deny the charge	sentence	

Noun (person)	Noun (crime/other)	Verb	Verb + noun phrases

2 Match some of the words in exercise 1 to these definitions.

1 someone who has suffered the effects of violence, illness or bad luck ....

2 get into a building illegally and steal things ....

3 give a punishment to someone who has committed a crime ....

4 the place where a judge decides whether someone is guilty of a crime ....

5 the action or crime of stealing something ....

6 do something that is considered wrong, or that is illegal ....

7 officially accuse someone of a crime ....

8 something that someone says or writes officially ....

9 say that you haven't done anything wrong ....

10 a person who sees an event happening, especially a crime or an accident ....

11 a group of people who listen to all the facts in a trial and decide whether a person is guilty or not guilty ....

12 think that someone may have committed a crime or done something bad ....

13 try to discover all the facts about something, especially a crime or an accident ....

14 a person who accesses other people's or organisations' computers illegally ....

3 Complete the sentences with words from exercise 1.

1 The police have .... one man with the .... of a number of bicycles from the local school.

2 Our house was .... last night – it's the first time we have been .... of a crime.

3 The bank robber was .... to eight years in prison.

4 Fortunately, several people .... the accident and said that it wasn't my fault.

5 We are .... the case at the moment, but haven't made an .... yet.

6 When the case was heard in .... yesterday, the .... of twelve people decided the burglar was guilty, and the .... ordered him to pay a fine.

7 Our TV, computer and hi-fi were all stolen in the ....

8 Over 50% of prisoners go on to .... more crimes after they have been .... from prison.

9 I was shocked when I was accused of being a computer .... – I'm useless with computers!

10 The police .... that the man was the .... of several other houses in the street.

READING

1 Read the article on page 77 quickly. Which of the crimes below do you think would *not* be tried in a teen court?

dropping litter ☐
hacking into government computers ☐
shoplifting ☐
burglary ☐
writing graffiti ☐

2 Find a word in the article which means the following.

d........................... **(n)** the person in a court who is accused of a **crime**

3 **Read the article again. Choose the correct answers.**

1 Defendants in teen courts
  A usually deny the charges.
  B volunteer to have their cases heard.
  C have not committed serious crimes.

2 The people who run the teen courts are
  A trained teenagers.
  B previous offenders.
  C adult experts.

3 The sentences given by a teen court
  A vary a lot.
  B can include a time in prison.
  C always involve community service.

4 What does *they* refer to in line 27?
  A the victims of a crime
  B the courts
  C the offenders

5 According to Simon Baxter, teen courts are successful because
  A they deliver appropriate punishments.
  B they help offenders understand their actions.
  C teenage court staff are well trained.

6 In comparison with adult courts, teen courts
  A tend to have a better reoffending rate.
  B tend to have a worse reoffending rate.
  C are less interested in the victim.

TEEN COURTS

Teen courts are a unique and successful way of dealing with teenage criminals. They provide an alternative to the traditional adult courts. Young people from the ages of 10 to 18 have their cases heard, and are sentenced at these courts – as long as their crime is not very serious.

Teen courts are run and staffed by young volunteers, who are trained in their roles by adult experts. These volunteers usually come from local high schools or youth organisations. The judge in a teen court does not usually have to decide if someone is guilty or not guilty, because most of the defendants do not deny the charges against them. The role of the teen court is simply to decide on an appropriate sentence for the crime. Sometimes the sentence is decided by a jury.

Sentences often involve the defendant being ordered to do something to help the person or people harmed by their crime. This can include writing formal apologies to the victim, doing some work to help repair damage, etc. Another common sentence is known as 'community service', in which the offender must perform tasks which

benefit the community such as picking up litter, or helping in a care home. Often the offender is also required to serve on a teen court jury.

The whole process, from charging to sentencing, helps to bring the young offender to an understanding of their
27 offence, and how it affects other people. **They** are frequently faced with the victim of their crime – an act that brings them face to face with the reality of what they have done. Offenders are made to feel responsible for their actions. Furthermore, by serving on a teen court jury, the offender is brought back into the system as an active member.

Simon Baxter, 16, who has been a teen court judge for two years, speaks about the success of the scheme: 'It's not about guilt or innocence or even punishment,' he says. 'It's about teenage offenders being shown what harm they did by people their own age. It's much more powerful when people of your own age and background tell you that you did wrong, rather than adults – although it does take some training to work well.'

And it does work. Evidence suggests that fewer than 5% of offenders whose cases are heard in teen courts go on to commit another crime. This compares to a 20% reoffending rate among those who go to adult courts. Not only that, teen courts also focus more on making things better for the victim, and the guilty offender does not end up with a criminal record – so everybody ends up better off in the long run.

EP **Word profile** *back*

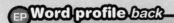

Complete the sentences with the words in the box.

> again   in 2012   in surprise
> of the queue   seat

1 I jumped back .... when the bird flew in through the kitchen window.
2 My brother gets ill if he sits on the back .... of the bus.
3 Back .... , we went to Hawaii on holiday.
4 It was hard to get our normal life back .... after the burglary.
5 Please go to the back .... and wait your turn.

GRAMMAR Modals of deduction: Past

1 Choose the correct modal verbs.

1 You were very lucky. You *might / must* have been seriously hurt!
2 Nobody is answering the door. They *couldn't / must* have gone out.
3 The burglar *couldn't / might* have known we were on holiday, because we didn't tell anybody.
4 I'm not sure, but I think I *might / must* have forgotten to lock the front door.
5 You *couldn't / must* have heard the news! Everybody's talking about it.
6 Marie *might / can't* have forgotten about the extra practice, because I reminded her about it.
7 I don't know who phoned, but it *must / could* have been Harry.
8 It *couldn't / must* have been very cold last night because there's ice on the roads this morning.

2 Complete the dialogues with a modal verb + *have* + the past participle of the verb in brackets.

1 **A:** Thanks for all your help. I

....

(fix) the broken door without you.

B: No problem. I think the burglar

....

(be) very strong.

2 **A:** It's possible that the police

....

(find) the criminal by now.

B: No, they ....
(find) him yet. They don't work that fast!

3 **A:** Do you think Steve

....

(get) stuck in traffic? He's very late.

B: No, he ....
(get) stuck in traffic – the streets aren't busy at this time.

A: Then you ....
(forget) to invite him. There's no other explanation!

4 **A:** I'm not sure, but I think I

....

(upset) Sophie when I told her how surprised I was that she got 100% in the test.

B: She ....
(get) 100%. That was a really hard test.
She ....
(be) lying to you.

5 **A:** Have you seen Gary recently? He's got some great news!

B: Well, I thought I saw him at the gym yesterday evening, but it

.... (be) him.

A: No, you .... (see) him yesterday evening, because he was with me, telling me his news.

3 Rewrite the sentences, using the word in brackets.

1 Perhaps Greg forgot to lock his bicycle. (might)
Greg might have ....
....

2 I'm sure it was really frightening to find a mouse in your bedroom. (been)
It ....
....

3 It's possible that they were too late for the early train. (missed)
They ....
....

4 I'm certain that it wasn't a very pleasant experience. (unpleasant)
It ....
....

4 ⊙ Correct the mistakes in these sentences or put a tick (✔) by any you think are correct.

1 The line-up was changed and that was the worst surprise I could have. ....
2 I spent almost an hour waiting, and then decided that the call could have been a joke.
....
3 I must have been seven years old at that time.
....
4 He could have triumph over the fish because of his knowledge of the sea. ....
5 Mark and Angela understood that he mustn't had told her the story. ....

VOCABULARY Negative prefixes

1 Write the opposites of these adjectives.

1 ......accurate	8 ......polite
2 ......expensive	9 ......popular
3 ......fair	10 ......possible
4 ......honest	11 ......reliable
5 ......legal	12 ......visible
6 ......organised	13 ......willing
7 ......patient	

2 Match some of the negative adjectives to their meanings.

1 not wanting to do something   ....
2 not able to be trusted or depended on   ....
3 rude   ....
4 too difficult to do   ....
5 likely to lie or do something criminal   ....
6 against the law   ....
7 not correct or exact   ....
8 not able to plan things well   ....
9 easily annoyed by mistakes or delays   ....
10 not possible to see   ....

WRITING   A persuasive email

See Prepare to write box, Student's Book page 67.

1 **Look at the task below. How many questions does the email contain?**

....

> You have received this email from your penfriend, Don.
>
> > The local police have set up a 'teen court'
> > in my town, and now they are looking for
> > volunteers to staff it. I have been asked to
> > join as a judge. What do you think about teen
> > courts? Are they a good idea? Should I join?
> > Looking forward to your reply.
> > Don Bradley

2 **Read the reply and answer the questions.**

1 What positive things does the writer say about teen courts?

....

....

2 Why does the writer believe that they are successful?

....

....

3 Why does the writer think it is a good idea to get involved?

....

....

> Hi Don
> We've had a teen court in our town for two
> years, and I can say without a doubt that it has
> improved things here a lot. Crime rates have
> fallen significantly, and those who commit
> a crime seldom commit another one after
> going to teen court.
> I firmly believe that they work so well because
> they make offenders face up to the reality of
> what they did. When they come face to face
> with the people affected by their crime, they
> truly understand why they were wrong. Most
> people would agree that is a very good thing.
> I'm convinced that you would benefit
> enormously by becoming a judge in a teen
> court. The training you will get is excellent,
> and you will feel like an active and useful
> member of the community. Not only that, but
> you'll get valuable experience which could
> help you find a good job later in life.
> All in all, teen courts are a great idea.
> They reduce crime and provide valuable
> opportunities to everyone who takes part.
> I say go for it!

3 **Read the email again.**

1 Underline four expressions which emphasise the writer's opinion.

2 Circle four adverbs which make verbs stronger.

4 **Read the task below. Tick (✔) what the task is asking you to do.**

define 'community service' ☐
give your understanding of what it is ☐
give your opinion on community service ☐
describe what prison is ☐
compare community service and prison in
some ways ☐

> You have received this email from your English
> penfriend.
>
> > I'm doing a project at school about
> > 'community service' as a punishment. What
> > do you know about this? Is it a more effective
> > way than prison to deal with young offenders?
> > Please let me know your opinion.
> > Thanks!
> > Tonya Gambaudo

5 **Write the points below into the correct column, then add two or three ideas of your own.**

> a waste of time
> contributes to society
> offenders still free to commit crime
> offenders locked away safely

	Community service	Prison
Good points		
Bad points		

6 **Write a reply to the email in exercise 4 in 140–190 words. Use your notes in exercise 5 and some expressions from exercise 3.**

VOCABULARY Places and feelings

1 Match the words from the box to the descriptions.

> cloth   concrete   construction   hut   shelter   tools

1 This is a small wooden building that you find in the mountains, for example. ....
2 This is anywhere you can go to escape from the rain, for example while you're waiting for a bus. ....
3 This is a very hard material used in building. It is sometimes used as the surface of roads. ....
4 These are objects we use to make things. A hammer is an example of one of these. ....
5 We use this for making clothes, sheets, curtains and so on. ....
6 This is another word for *building*. ....

2 Complete the sentences with the best words in the box.

> breathtaking   dissatisfied   magical   passionate   relaxed   weird

1 I'm not at all happy with the game of tennis I just played. I'm feeling ....
2 Somebody just said something very strange to me. It was a .... thing to say.
3 That gymnastic display almost had a physical effect on me. It was ....
4 Dan feels strongly about his favourite football team. He's .... about them.
5 When you're a child, the world can seem beautiful and exciting. It's a .... time.
6 We always have a very informal time when we visit our friends in America. It's a .... atmosphere.

3 Choose the correct answers.

1 My sister is very *passionate* / *relaxed* about architecture, and she's going to study it at university.
2 The new theatre is made partly of *construction* / *concrete*. It's really ugly.
3 The wonderful view from the top of the Eiffel Tower was *weird* / *breathtaking*.
4 The meal was so small that I felt very *relaxed* / *dissatisfied* when it was finished.
5 Everyone enjoyed the party because the atmosphere was very *passionate* / *relaxed*.
6 Do you need a specific *tool* / *cloth* to take the wheel off the bike?

READING

1 Quickly read the text about teenagers and shopping malls. Choose the best title.

a The perfect teen hang-out   b A revolution in shopping   c The problem of teens in shopping malls

2 Choose the answer (A, B, C or D) which you think fits best according to the text.

1 The author thinks teens see shopping malls as places
  A to buy clothes.
  B to spend time with their family.
  C to meet their friends.
  D to work.

2 Younger teenagers hang out in shopping malls more than older teens because
  A they don't have to drive there.
  B they have nowhere else to go.
  C they have part-time jobs there.
  D they have more leisure time.

3 What does the psychology professor think about teens hanging out in shopping malls?
  A concerned that it is slowing their development
  B worried that they are not using their time productively
  C happy that there is a safe place for them to go
  D optimistic about the academic benefits

4 What does the word *scarce* mean in line 25?
  A regular
  B rare
  C desirable
  D expensive

5 Why is the author sometimes treated badly by shop staff?
  A Because she acts wild.
  B Because the shop staff judge all teenagers to be the same.
  C Because teenagers are not allowed in the shops.
  D Because shop staff are unhappy with their jobs.

6 According to the author, what makes the shopping mall so attractive?
  A the freedom from adult control
  B the opportunities for bad behaviour
  C the safety of the environment
  D the availability of good shops

The role of the mall in teen life

I went to the mall at the weekend and started to think about what it means to us. You know what it's like. You ask your mum to drive you down to the shopping mall so that you can hang out with your friends and she says, 'Of course. We can do some shopping together!' Er, no, Mum. I want you to drive me to the shopping mall, *and then leave me alone!*

The thing is, shopping malls have become the place for us teens to hang out. There are a number of reasons for that – we've looked at it on my psychology course. I was surfing the web for an essay when I read this quote from a psychology professor at a British university: 'Adults see malls as somewhere they go to do shopping, whereas teenagers go to there to socialise.'

Interesting. She also says that hanging out at the shopping mall is most popular in the early teens, up to about 15. That's obvious – reasons being that older teens are likely to be able to go to other places, they can drive, they often have part-time jobs so they have some money. However, for younger teens like me, the mall becomes a cool place to hang out.

This professor also said that because some towns don't have any places for teens – no youth clubs, no parks, no safe spaces at all, then hanging out at the mall can be an important part of teenage development. You know, a shopping mall is a safe place to meet, to talk, and to deal with the complicated issues of getting along with your friends.

She's right. I don't need any money to go to the shopping mall. If I want to go to the swimming pool or the cinema with my friends, it costs money – and, as you can imagine, money's pretty **scarce** for kids my age! My mother doesn't really worry too much about my choice of hang-out, because she knows I'm a fairly responsible teenager. 'If you tell me that you and your friends are always polite to the people who work there, I believe you. If you're well behaved, nobody will mind you hanging around the place too much.'

This is another quote from the web: 'Very few teenagers get into trouble at the shopping mall. But you have to be careful, because the opportunities for bad behaviour are all there. Although there is no direct adult supervision, which is what makes the place so attractive in the first place, the presence of adult shoppers and security guards does act as a controlling factor.'

On the other hand, when a few teens do behave badly, it can mean that all of us get treated with suspicion. My friends and I are sometimes treated rudely by shop staff. Just because some other teenagers did some pretty awful things about a year ago, people think we're all like that. It's not exactly fair.

But, of course, we deal with it. Dealing with things is part of growing up, right? The main thing is that our parents understand that the shopping mall is where we go to get away from them. The last thing we want is for them to make us feel awkward in front of our friends. So, Mum, if you see me in the shopping mall, don't be surprised if I ignore you!

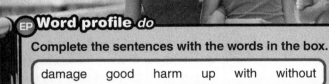

EP Word profile *do*

Complete the sentences with the words in the box.

| damage | good | harm | up | with | without |

1 You'll do yourself .... if you aren't careful.
2 I'm going to do .... my bedroom with the money I got from working this summer.
3 That's interesting, but it has nothing to do .... our project.
4 You can complain if you want, but it won't do you any ....
5 You're going to help with the school play, aren't you? We can't do .... you!
6 I did some really bad .... to my bike when I hit the tree.

GRAMMAR -ing forms; participle clauses

1 Match the beginnings and endings of the sentences.

1 Choosing to study English ....
2 I really enjoy ....
3 I learnt how to cook ....
4 I never get anxious ....
5 Falling off my scooter ....
6 Sometimes I'm just not capable of ....

a was the best decision I ever made.
b from watching my mother.
c didn't hurt as much as you might think.
d about doing exams.
e watching our cats play together.
f making difficult decisions.

2 Write sentences using these words.

0 I / learn / how to play this game / by / watch / my brother
  I learnt how to play this game by watching my brother.

1 Tonya / be tired of / live / in a small house

2 the kids / enjoy / play / in their tree house yesterday

3 ride / a bicycle / is a good way / of / keep / fit

4 I / not be / capable of / fix this computer

5 you shouldn't / feel anxious about / speak / to the class

6 by / save / her pocket money / she was able to buy a bike

3 Rewrite the sentences to start with an *-ing* form.

0 It can be dangerous to jump into the swimming pool.
  Jumping into the pool can be dangerous.

1 We aren't allowed to run in the corridors.

2 It's boring to live in the countryside.

3 It's useful to speak another language.

4 It's necessary to drive a car to get around here.

5 It's cool to hang out with friends at the shopping mall.

4 Rewrite the sentences with a suitable participle to replace the underlined words. You may have to change the word order.

0 <u>Simon was listening</u> to music and he didn't hear the phone.
  Listening to music, Simon didn't hear the phone.

1 <u>When she spoke to Marco</u>, she discovered they went to the same gym.

2 On the way home I saw a man <u>who was sleeping on a bench</u>.

3 My dad's office, <u>which has no air conditioning</u>, is very hot in the summer.

4 <u>I felt embarrassed</u> and I left the room.

5 My mobile phone <u>had no power</u> and so didn't work.

6 Nuria <u>waited for an hour for Andrea</u>, and she wondered why she was still her friend.

7 I looked at all the phones and decided to buy the one <u>which offered the best features</u>.

8 <u>Because he didn't understand one question</u>, Eric failed the test.

5 ⊙ Correct the mistakes in these sentences or put a tick (✔) by any you think are correct.

1 I'm looking forward to go there. ....
2 Thank you for writing to me. ....
3 Nowadays to go to work is a bit complicated because of the cars and the busy streets.
....
4 First of all, I think that drive 100 kilometres on Sunday is too far. ....
5 I went out with my friends to celebrate my birthday after have dinner in a well-known restaurant. ....

VOCABULARY Compound adjectives ending in *-ing*

1 Match 1–7 to a–g to make compound adjectives.

1	cost-	**a**	threatening
2	eye-	**b**	catching
3	heart-	**c**	consuming
4	life-	**d**	cutting
5	mouth-	**e**	watering
6	record-	**f**	breaking
7	time-	**g**	warming

1 .... 2 .... 3 .... 4 .... 5 .... 6 .... 7 ....

2 Write the correct compound adjective next to its meaning.

1 causing feelings of pleasure and happiness ....

2 reducing the amount of money spent ....

3 taking up many hours ....

4 better, faster, more, etc. than anything before ....

5 causing danger of death ....

6 looking or smelling as if it is going to taste really good ....

7 very noticeable ....

LISTENING

1 ▶13 Listen to five conversations. Match the conversations to the pictures.

2 Read the questions in exercise 3. Underline the most important points.

3 ▶13 Listen again and choose the correct answers, A, B or C.

1 You hear two friends talking about a clothes shop. What does the boy think his friend will dislike about it?
   A the price of the clothes there
   B the people who work there
   C the music they play there

2 You hear a girl talking on the phone to her father. What is the purpose of her call?
   A to request some help
   B to apologise for being late
   C to borrow some money

3 You hear a man and a woman talking on the radio. What point is the man making about life in the 21st century?
   A People are lucky to have lots of things to do.
   B People seldom relax properly.
   C People are too easily frightened.

4 You hear a boy and a girl talking in a café. They agree that
   A the place looks good.
   B the drinks are really good.
   C it is expensive.

5 You hear a boy and a girl talking about a short trip in a boat. What does the boy say about the trip?
   A It was too expensive.
   B It was too scary.
   C It was too long.

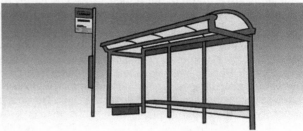

a ....

b ....

c ....

d ....

e ....

Acknowledgements

Development of this publication has made use of the Cambridge English Corpus, a multi-billion word collection of spoken and written English. It includes the Cambridge Learner Corpus, a unique collection of candidate exam answers. Cambridge University Press has built up the Cambridge English Corpus to provide evidence about language use that helps to produce better language teaching materials.

This product is informed by English Profile, a Council of Europe-endorsed research programme that is providing detailed information about the language that learners of English know and use at each level of the Common European Framework of Reference (CEFR). For more information, please visit www.englishprofile.org

The authors and publishers acknowledge the following sources of copyright material and are grateful for the permissions granted. While every effort has been made, it has not always been possible to identify the sources of all the material used, or to trace all copyright holders. If any omissions are brought to our notice, we will be happy to include the appropriate acknowledgements on reprinting.

The Prospect for the abridged extract on p. 5 'Tips for how to be an awesome new kid at school, by Jacinda Sicori, *The Prospect* 14/06/2013; The Department of Health for the adapted extract on p. 25 from 'Healthy eating for teens' http://www.nhs.uk/Livewell/Goodfood/Pages/healthy-eating-teens.aspx Contains public sector information licensed under the Open Government Licence v2.0; The Department of Health for the adapted extract on p. 25 from 'Healthy eating tips' http://www.nhs.uk/Livewell/Goodfood/Pages/healthy-eating-teens.aspx Contains public sector information licensed under the Open Government Licence v3.0; NBC News for the adapted extract on p. 33 'Are we nearly there yet? Family travels the world for 11 years?' by Harriet Baskas, *NBC News* 06/04/2011; Adapted extract on p. 37 'Amazing (very) young entrepreneurs' by Nicole Fallon, *Business News Daily* 05/09/2013 Copyrighted 2014. TechMedia Network. 112843:1114AT; Yahoo for the adapted extract on p. 53 'Playstation motor racing genius earns chance to drive for Red Bull's F1 team,' by Caroline Macleod-Smith, 19/02/2014, reprinted with permission from Yahoo. © 2014 Yahoo; Adapted extract on p. 65 'Top ten surprising results of global warming', by Live Science staff, *Live Science* 16/10/2011 Copyrighted 2014.TechMedia Network. 113255:1114AT; The Independent for the adapted extract on p. 69 'Has Banksy's real identity been discovered at last?' by Robert Verkaik, *The Independent* 14/07/2008.

Photo acknowledgements

p. 4: Picture Partners/Alamy; p. 5: Steve Debenport/Getty; p.7: David Crausby/Alamy; p. 8: Kuttig – People/Alamy; p. 11: Stanislav Halcin/Alamy; p. 12: (T/L) Clive Brunskill/Getty, (T/R) Bettmann/Corbis, (B/L) Patrick Branwell Bronte/Getty, (B/R) Christian Bertrand/Shutterstock; p. 17: Andy Clark/Reuters/Corbis; p. 19 (T) Fotosr52/Shutterstock, (T/M) Douglas Peebles Photography/Alamy, (B/M) Global Warming Images/Alamy, (B) Naypong/Shutterstock; p. 25: Peter Vrabel/Shutterstock; p. 27: (T/L) Alex Segre/Getty, (T/R) wavebreakmedia/Shutterstock, (B/L) Petroos/Shutterstock, (B/R) AnnaIA/Shutterstock; p. 29: (T) RubberBall/Alamy, (B) Chris Rout/Alamy; p. 33: Gallo images/Alamy; p. 35: Image Source/Alamy; p. 36: (T) Ballda/Shutterstock, (T/M) al1962/Shutterstock, (M/L) Sam72/Shutterstock, (M/R) dmytro herasymeniuk/Shutterstock, (B) Africa Studio/Shutterstock; p. 39: (T) Hannamariah/Shutterstock, (B) Blend Images/Alamy; p. 44: (T/L) quinky/Shutterstock, (T/R) 4X-image/Getty, (B/L) Andrey Stenkin/Getty, (B/R) Science & Society Picture Library/Getty; p. 49: S_L/Shutterstock; p. 51: Anthony Lee/Getty; p. 53: (T/L) Darrell Ingham/Getty, (B/R) Brian Cleary/Getty; p. 55: ZUMA Press, Inc/Alamy; p. 60: James R Clarke/Alamy; p. 65: (T) Lukasz Anyst/Shutterstock, (T/M) think4photop/Shutterstock, (B/M) Rob Bayer/Shutterstock, (B/L) ER_09/Shutterstock, (B) mffoto/Shutterstock; p. 67: JPL Designs/Shutterstock; p. 9: John Farnham/Alamy; p. 71: Lewis Tse Pui Lung/Shutterstock; p. 73: Fuse/Getty; p. 75: (L) tomborro/Alamy, (R) valzan/Shutterstock; p. 77: ZUMA Press, Inc/Alamy; p. 79: Marc Asnin/Corbis; p. 81: (T/L) ESTUDI M6/Shutterstock; (B) Picturenet/Getty.

Front cover photograph by Lucky Business/Shutterstock.

Illustrations

Mark Duffin p. 21; Kevin Hopgood (Beehive Illustration) pp. 16, 31, 43, 83; Rory Walker pp. 41, 57, 58, 59, 62.

The publishers are grateful to the following contributors: text design and layouts: emc design Ltd; cover design: Andrew Ward; picture research: emc design Ltd; audio recordings: produced by IH Sound and recorded at DSound, London; edited by Diane Hall.